Sunday Times best-selling author Michele Knight-Waite has been a well-known Tarot reader, psychic, manifester, and astrologer for decades. She often jokes that she was born with a pack of Tarot cards in her hands.

Michele grew up in a tempestuous environment with a wild Italian psychic mother. Tarot cards were her playthings. Her childhood was traumatic and dangerous, and Tarot became the treasure map that led her out of her wounded beginnings. She eventually left home at 13, with Tarot as her constant guide and companion.

Voted the UK's Favourite Psychic several years running by readers of *Soul & Spirit* – one of the UK's leading magazines in the mind, body, and spirit genre, Michele recently starred as the astrology expert in the Discovery+ show *Written in the Stars*.

She lives and works in Devon, in a castle overlooking the sea with her wife Cathy. She continues to manifest, helping others on a similar path of recovery and self-belief. She is surrounded by dogs and rescue donkeys and horses, and a Tarot pack is still in her hands – this time one of her own creation.

For your free interactive Celtic Cross Tarot reading and more about my Tarot deck visit **www.knightwaitetarot.com**

For a reading with one of my brilliant psychics and hundreds of articles on everything from psychic ability to manifesting as well as heaps of free readings, go to **www.micheleknight.com**, or for all things astrological – including free birth and compatibility charts – go to **www.horoscope.co.uk**

THE
Knight - Waite
TAROT
GUIDEBOOK

Meanings & Readings

MICHELE KNIGHT - WAITE

JOHN MURRAY

First published by John Murray One in 2023
An imprint of John Murray Press
A division of Hodder & Stoughton Ltd,
An Hachette UK company

1

A CIP catalogue record for this title is available from the British Library

Hardback ISBN 978 1 399 80736 4
eBook ISBN 978 1 399 80737 1

Printed in China by C&C Offset Printing Co., Ltd.

John Murray Press policy is to use papers that are natural, renewable and
recyclable products and made from wood grown in sustainable forests.
The logging and manufacturing processes are expected to conform to the
environmental regulations of the country of origin.

John Murray Press
Carmelite House
50 Victoria Embankment
London EC4Y 0DZ

www.johnmurraypress.co.uk

Dedicated to my wife, Cathy Knight-Waite,
the full moon over the ocean of my heart.

CONTENTS

HELLO, GORGEOUS SOUL   1

DIVING DEEP INTO THE TAROT   3

MAJOR ARCANA   6

The Fool   8
The Magician   10
The High Priestess   12
The Empress   14
The Emperor   16
The Hierophant   18
The Lovers (three cards)   20
The Chariot   24
Strength   26
The Hermit   28
The Wheel of Fortune   30
Justice   32
The Hanged One   34
Death   36
Temperance   38
The Devil   40
The Tower   42
The Star   44
The Moon (two cards)   46
The Sun   48
Judgement   50
The World   52

MINOR ARCANA   54

Wands   56
Cups   76
Swords   96
Pentacles   116

COURT CARDS   136

Wands   138
Cups   146
Swords   154
Pentacles   162

SAMPLE SPREADS   171

OUR TAROT SUPERSTARS   216

ACKNOWLEDGEMENTS   229

HELLO, GORGEOUS SOUL

A huge welcome to the Knight-Waite Tarot.

I often say I was born with a deck of Tarot in my hands. My mother was a psychic Tarot reader, so the cards were my childhood playthings. The Tarot was my constant companion, my guide, my lifelong savior, and without a doubt the compass I used to create my future. Of all the decks, the Rider–Waite–Smith has always been my most beloved. I see the Knight-Waite Tarot as a reimagining of this iconic deck and my love letter to the Rider–Waite–Smith deck, specifically to Pamela Colman-Smith, the illustrator.

The fabulous maverick Pamela Colman-Smith was an all-round remarkable soul: half Jamaican, queer, a Suffragette, and an artist who was way ahead of her time. Perhaps the reason why the Rider–Waite–Smith is the most popular Tarot deck of all time is because Pamela hid her magic in plain sight.

I wanted to do this project because, although I have the most profound respect for the Rider–Waite–Smith and other original Tarot cards, I've also felt genuine frustration with their lack of diversity. Because the original decks were created in a time of even deeper oppression, they don't honor different sexualities and gender expressions, and are generally white-centric. I think Pamela would have approved of a more inclusive vision, which is what led me on the journey to create this deck and to carry her vision on into a new, more inclusive age.

Pamela gave this essential advice, advice which has stood the test of time and remains one of the best approaches to accessing the full wisdom of the Tarot:

'After you have found how to tell a simple story, put in more details . . . Learn from everything, see everything, and above all feel everything! . . . Find eyes within, look for the door into the unknown country.'

So, who else could I have chosen to be the High Priestess in my pack other than Pamela herself? She's right here guarding the wisdom while drawing back the curtain to the mysteries held within us all. I've included other spellbinding historical characters who have either been minimized, written out of history, or lost in the mists of time. The characters of these cards are encouraging us to unleash our unique free spirit via their own incredible soul journeys.

Tarot uses a symbolic language that tugs at our unconscious, dragging to the surface both treasure and truths as we enter that 'unknown country' that lies between what we know and what we intuit. It empowers and enlightens us to the answers already inside us. I've consciously created a deck to not only help you connect with the symbolic meaning of the cards but to inspire your intuition.

Why is this deck called the Knight-Waite Tarot? Just like the Wheel of Fortune's magic, a strange twist of fate in 2014 brought my extraordinary wife, Cathy Waite, to me. We married at the start of the pandemic in 2020, which coincided with my completion of this deck, and I became Michele Knight-Waite.

You might notice that I'm the Magician, Empress, and Death Cards. These are all doorways we pass through on our soul's journey. We are in an endless dance of life, death, rebirth, co-creation. Hopefully these cards will be around long after me, and in a way, it's a whispered message and reminder of that endlessness. The Knight-Waite Tarot carries my heart, and I share it with you with the deepest love.

Michele Knight-Waite

DIVING DEEP INTO THE TAROT

The Tarot is an endless learning journey that has no beginning, middle, or end. Once you begin that journey, your Tarot cards are your constant companions. They will provide you with guidance, wisdom, and answers right when you need them. They will open the doors to your higher intuition and reveal astonishing truths about yourself, your life, and the people around you.

I've had the privilege of teaching people the Tarot for over 35 years, and it still astonishes and delights me that some people can pick up the deck and instantly read like a pro. Others may take longer to develop an affinity with the cards, but the truth is there's no 'right' or 'wrong' way to read them. The cards are just a gateway to our own psychic abilities. They link us to universal wisdom but it's our interpretation of them that leads to our greatest discoveries and builds our relationship to the cards.

The Tarot is the intersection of mysticism and quantum mechanics where we can gain a snapshot of our future or the knowledge we need, where we actively participate in co-creating our destiny with the Universe. That's one of the most compelling things about Tarot. That, coupled with the fact that you can never get bored with it. Because even if you wanted to learn everything about the Tarot, it would take you several lifetimes! As a wild Aries spirit, I know the value of jumping into things instantly. So I'm going to show you some swift and intuitive ways of learning to read the cards and to build that relationship with them quickly. Not only that, but you'll just as quickly gain confidence in your interpretive skills. So – let's begin.

Take a few moments to just hold your Tarot deck in your hands. Close your eyes and feel the weight of the cards. Know that within this deck, there is an opportunity to connect with your deepest wisdom and to uncover mysteries within and without. Feel the cards begin to warm in your hands with the thrill of possibilities ready to be explored as your relationship with them begins to grow. Building a unique connection to your deck leads to powerful readings and a deeper, more profound experience. Before we get into the interpretation, I want you to

EXPERIENCE the cards. A good Tarot reader will weave together signs and symbols to channel a multi-layered story. Each time they look at the cards, they will feel and experience something new, something unique to the moment, while still retaining the essence of the cards' message. The cards can express themselves in different ways symbolically, literally, and emotionally.

Now you're ready to begin. As you shuffle the cards, forget everything that you may know about the Tarot. And that includes the 'traditional' interpretations. Instead, be open to what's going to come. Pull out a card and say out loud the first impression you receive. Tune into your body. How does the card make you feel? Do you get a sense of pleasure, fear, or intrigue from the card? Does the card make you feel a specific sensation? Does a color, a thought, a feeling, or even a person spring to mind?

Write down the first thoughts you have on what the card means. Then expand on this and write a little one-paragraph story for what exactly is going on in the card. How does this card relate to your life right now? When you're ready, take another card and repeat the process. Do this with several cards and see what you pick up. Are these stories interlocking or related to someone or something specific? Are they an answer to a question or something happening in your life right now (whether you asked about this or not)?

Whatever you learn in the coming chapters, ALWAYS, in every reading, look at the card with new eyes. Don't listen to me or anyone else; listen to what the card feels like in the moment. Ironically, the less you try, the more you should flow and the more relevant it should be. That's the paradox and the promise of the Tarot for you.

Much love, Michele

P.S. A quick note about reversals. I tend not to use them in the traditional sense (i.e., when a card is upside-down) but allow my intuition to guide me on the message of the card in that moment. I can look at a card and sense when it's not being channeled or when the energy is reversed. Perhaps both energies exist and our job is to understand how it can be shifted into its highest expression.

For Tarot spreads, free Tarot readings, and a deeper dive into this deck, come and visit me at **www.knightwaitetarot.com** or **www.micheleknight.com**

MAJOR ARCANA

THE MAGIC IN THE DECK

THE FOOL

Unlimited Possibility, Childlike Wonder, Freedom

'The Fool is a spark of the stars in your infinite heart, calling you to tumble into the unknown – curiosity, your sturdy parachute gliding you to another soul location. Boundless potential is woven in trust, all-knowing, innocent and free.'

Behold the glorious Fool! The Fool is arguably the most powerful card in the Tarot as it's similar to a magical dice: it leads you to the entire deck and a world of unlimited possibility. It's pure magic on a stick! The Fool calls for a leap of faith, to try things differently and dive headlong into new experiences which can transform our soul path instantly. The Fool is everything and nothing. The Fool trusts and knows the cycle of life is just a game, that whatever situation they land in they will learn and they will be safe. They have the pure heart of a child and the wisdom of the ancients.

When the Fool turns up in your Tarot reading, an opportunity will appear. It's time to be spontaneous and embrace the unknown. Listen to the call of your wild heart and be open to doing things you've never done before. By taking that brave first step, a new path unfolds right in front of you. Trust in the moment and believe in your ability to adapt and thrive. The Fool urges us to fearlessly throw ourselves into a fresh chapter.

Reversed

Reversed, the Fool tells us: look before you leap. If you jump, where will you land? Time to trust your intuition and to avoid being reckless or self-destructive.

We all know the difference between acting in good faith and doing something that will have terrible consequences. Don't attempt to enter into a situation that you know will be a disaster. Ask yourself: is there another way, another possibility I can choose?

THE MAGICIAN

Manifestation, Empowerment, Awakening

'One hand reaching into the multiverse channeling a lighting strike of possibility. You're an alchemist with magic in your fingertips. And so it begins. Onwards!'

The Magician signals a new cycle of self-creation. You're a Magician now and have all the tools in front of you to create your future. The key, of course, is to use them. A spark of enchantment is surging through your spirit. Your energy is a magic wand. Where will you point it? Where your focus goes, energy flows.

Own the four elements you need to conjure your dreams:

Fire = passion
Water = emotion, empathy, and intuition
Earth = practical skills
Air = intellect and ideas.

Add all of these ingredients together and you become an alchemist able to conjure self-created future, opportunity, and change. Pay close attention to your thoughts and beliefs; they play a large part in creating your reality. Your words are spells right now. Cast them wisely.

Reversed

Blocked energy?

Have you lost your faith? When we stop believing in ourselves, our inner magic grinds to a halt. Progress slows or stutters. The potential we once felt is missing. The dream – elusive. Reboot your quest with extreme self-nurturing and belief in your own magic. Reconnect to joy. It's time to treat yourself with the love and care you'd give your best friend. Self-belief begins with the ability to stop judging yourself and comparing your unique magic to others.

THE HIGH PRIESTESS

Intuition, Knowing, Guardian of Secrets

'Fearlessly enter the sacred garden of your intuition. Pass the pillars of truth through the curtain of self-belief. Wisdom and revelation dangle from every tree.'

The High Priestess sits on a throne of wisdom and knowing. Behind the curtain are all the answers you will ever need – expect a psychic awakening. Sacred mysteries will reveal themselves. Pay attention to your dreams, to strange synchronicities, and to the constant flutter of your intuition. Tap into your psychic ability and it becomes a superpower ever ready to advise you. Your intuition is rising. Your knowledge is vast, billowing in front of you in large font. Are you listening? Are you allowing yourself to trust in the unseen? You've reached a point of power and your unconscious is giving up her jewels. Listen closely to your dreams and to all of your gut feelings. The Crescent Moon at her feet says the wisdom of the Moon grounds you and gives you answers. The Moon can help you step into your unique rhythm. Your natural instincts are empowering instruments in your magical toolbox. It's time to acknowledge your own magnificence, to explore, swim, and plunge into the divine mysteries.

You already have the solutions or answers you seek. Just listen to your inner voice. *'Note the dress, the type of face; see if you can trace the character in the face; note the pose. . . . First watch the simple forms of joy, of fear, of sorrow; look at the position taken by the whole body. . . . After you have found how to tell a simple story, put in more details. . . . Learn from everything, see everything, and above all feel everything! . . . Find eyes within, look for the door into the unknown country.'* – Pamela Colman-Smith

Reversed

Sometimes, it can seem easier to kid ourselves than to accept reality. However, this can keep us in energetic and emotional limbo. What are you hiding from? Is it from the truth that your intuition is broadcasting loud and clear? It's time to listen to it and trust your gut feelings.

THE EMPRESS

Sensual, Abundant, Creative, Nurturing

'Nourish your Goddess heart, sway to the rhythm of your sensuality. Your divine spirit sparkles now, alight with opportunity and attraction. Creativity and abundance flourish knowing that fruitful fortunes draw near.'

The Empress urges us to examine, embrace, ground, and live in our creative centre. They rule by divine, open-hearted sensuality, magnetism, nurturing, power, and attraction – all effortlessly. Nothing is forced. The Empress attracts simply by tapping into her creative potential, pregnant with possibilities, relaxed and giving birth to ideas, energy, babies, and wild things. She's open, warm-hearted, and confident, secure in the knowledge that what she/they need comes to her effortlessly via the magical natural order of things.

The Empress is reminding you that you are a creator and that what is meant for you flows rather than needs to be forced.

Reversed

Do you feel disconnected from your power?

You may have felt that you've given all you have to offer. Perhaps someone has taken advantage of your nurturing and generous ways, or made you feel unworthy or unlovable. The Empress reversed is reminding you that your power and capacity to give and receive love are still intact.

You don't need to close down your energy or become angry and defensive. When you stand in your power and remember who you are when you love yourself and spend time recharging your creative juices, everything changes.

Reconnect to your centre.

THE EMPEROR

Boundaries, Will, Rulership

'Bravo, sweet warrior, you're reclaiming the power that was always yours. You are your own fearless protector, setting boundaries and galloping towards freedom using self-control.'

Our Emperor represents strong boundaries. Traditional Tarot often depicts this figure as authoritative, rigid, self-possessed, and controlling. Emperor energy can be an external force, not ruled by emotion, but by cold hard facts. In challenging situations, the Emperor appears to give unwavering authority and even protection.

If you find yourself dealing with an oppressor, an outside controlling force, or unwanted dominance, know that no one has power over your soul, your spirit, and who you are.

Connect to your inner protective ruler spirit, stand your ground, and, above all, channel self-control.

Reversed

Are you or is someone around you being too dominating or pedantic?

Control issues tend to come from fear. Seek support and pay attention to any coercive behaviour. If you find yourself being controlling, tell yourself it's okay to let go. Knowing you can't control anyone but yourself leads you to a place of greater freedom and joy. You're more than your ideas and beliefs.

Let go of the need to be right and embrace the right to be happy instead.

THE HIEROPHANT

THE HIEROPHANT

Structure, Society, Tradition

'Responsibility opens the gates to freedom. Craft your rules with the language of your heart. Feast on knowledge, knowing you are a reflection of the society you seek.'

The Hierophant talks to us of society's rules, structures, and learning. I used to have a block around this card until I realized that one of the fundamental building blocks of my success was laid when I learned to embrace order.

The Hierophant is coming to tell you that you have the opportunity to transform your life. Be curious, seek new ideas, and be questioning. Now is the time to create the foundations for your dreams to blossom and grow. Look out for a clue to the next step. Commit to your plans and fertilize your brilliance with structure!

The Hierophant is a reminder that we as individuals make up society, and our voices matter. Therefore, we must support equality and work towards a world where we are all free. We each have a part to play in transforming the world and not ignoring the oppression surrounding us, especially if we aren't directly experiencing it.

Reversed

It's time to shake up your belief system.

What beliefs are holding you back? Resist those that try to make you conform or deny your unique soul, and those that simply no longer hold true for you. Whose ideas are these anyway?

Time to question why you believe what you do. Don't let the past hijack your future.

THE LOVERS SPREAD OVER THREE CARDS

Passion, Choices, Love

'Love rolls in, bringing waves of choices. Listen to the answers, whispered deep within. Nourish longings, nurture passion. Remember, Love begins with loving you.'

The Lovers is all about choice, which is why I've given you more than one card to choose from. So, choose yours from the three given. Or leave all three in the pack and see which card chooses you. Don't just go by sexuality but the energy of the couples. One Lovers card represents romantic love, one passionate love, and the older couple commitment and security. If there's one universal message of this card, it is this: it's all Love.

The Lovers card shows us the importance of self-love and healing to be fully equipped to deal with the relationships that will cross our path. Love is one of the key lessons on our soul's voyage, and it begins within us. Whenever the Lovers card shows up, it speaks to us of choice. There are two paths ahead. Choose with your heart.

The good news is that by receiving the Lovers card, there's a promise of renewed passion. Passion can take many forms. You might find yourself falling in love, or perhaps you fall in love with your partner all over again. You could fall for an inspirational project that makes your heart sing. Or simply fall in love with your own life, paving the way for more love to enter. Enjoy it, trust it, and share it!

Reversed

Do you currently lack self-love? Are you in a relationship that doesn't honor you? When we improve our relationship with ourselves, it spreads to all our relationships – past, present, and potential. This card can indicate a fear of commitment. Yours or another's? Look to whether you repeatedly fall in love with people who are unavailable, or your relationship status reads 'it's complicated'. Look out for an emotional connection that is not all that it seems.

THE LOVERS

THE CHARIOT

Movement, Action, Will

'Souldier, your Chariot awaits, your thoughts 10,000 starlings, a murmuration of movement carrying you on. The more aligned you are, the faster you'll fly, each positive belief a jewel in your breastplate.'

Prepare yourself! Things are starting to move very quickly, and that momentum has a direction that's all its own! Because sphinxes and not horses pull the Chariot, we know that a spiritual force forward is leading the way.

The fuel for our life, the Chariot is our thoughts and beliefs, our determination, and our inner strength. When we change routines, patterns, and destructive ways of thinking, we liberate ourselves and fine-tune our spiritual engine. Your purpose is victory, and the key to achieving it is bringing all your different and conflicting inner energies together and channeling them instead of being led by them. There is a difference! Time to banish self-sabotage and doubt.

Your remarkable spirit deserves to unleash the full force of your magnificence. Channel this blast of energy. You are in control of your primal essence – not by blocking it, controlling it, or imprisoning it, but by bringing all the facets of yourself together. Face forward, fearless and unstoppable. You are working in harmony, and through this, you can take great strides forward. Don't let anyone divert you from your path. Onwards!

Reversed

Are you your own worst enemy? Fighting with yourself? Is there a fear of success or change? It's time to dive deep into your worries and see what obstacles you're putting up to prevent your progress. Instead, embrace the parts of you that you've been taught to see as fears, flaws, faults, or simply being 'not quite good enough'. In them lie your power, strength, and beauty. Recover them now to reboot your authentic self.

STRENGTH

Power, Energy, Protection

'The lion within awakens, your beacon of power burns bright, courage your torch, leading you gently onwards.'

Beloved, you are protected now. There have been times when you didn't know how it would turn out, when life tumbled into chaos, when your heart shattered into a million tiny pieces. But guess what?

YOU MADE IT. And you emerged stronger than before.

You have a core potency that's rising to the surface now. Your courage is about to bring you great gifts. Remember, Strength is not angry or ferocious; Strength allows for compassion and for tenderness, especially towards ourselves. Be gentle with yourself. Honor your courage and your victories. If you're facing a challenge right now, understand that Strength means coming from a place of self-love first and Strength is with you.

Reversed

There may be feelings of chaos or a fear of losing control. Pay attention to your inner voice or any self-destructive patterns. Trust in your spirit and path. Is someone forcing an issue? If you've given your power away, it's time to take it back.

THE HERMIT

Solitude, Wisdom, Enlightenment

'Solitude unwraps your gifts and spins spells of possibility. The knowledge curled within you, once illuminated, sprouts wings of freedom.'

What you resist persists. The Hermit is a call to unplug, to de-stress, to spend time in reflection. If you've felt lonely or lost recently, the Hermit brings a beacon of hope, a guiding light which is always found within us. It's high time to reassess, recover, and access the wisdom within. Equally, if you've been stressed out, run ragged, or not had a minute to yourself, the Hermit calls for a timeout.

Self-care involves a little peace and taking back your inner space. Use this opportunity to embrace stillness. At the same time, it's a golden moment to connect with the bottomless resource of your profound inner knowledge.

The light of insight guides you and pierces the darkness. Clarity replaces confusion. Deep within you, you have an unlimited source of awareness and power.

Reversed

The upside-down Hermit suggests a lack of trust and a disconnect from your own inner wisdom.

Do you trust your instincts? Are you lonely or isolated? Or does sticking to your inner truth put you 'out on a limb'? Whatever situation you're in can be remedied by renewing faith in your intuition. Deep down, you have the answers. That small voice that whispers your truth.

THE WHEEL OF FORTUNE

Fate, Change, Soul Cycle

'Roll up, roll up, the wheel of life spins you into unexpected outcomes. A twist of fate with thrilling shifts diverts your soul path.'

The Wheel of Fortune turns in your favour like the needle on a compass pointing to a significant life change ahead. A profound experience is on the way. Although we have free will, there are sprinklings of 'destiny-driven' events, meetings, and people that bring a turn of fortune or a fork in the road of our soul journey. Seemingly insignificant coincidences and synchronicities or what we think of as 'luck' can spin our lives in an exciting new direction.

The Wheel of Fortune sets life-transforming events in motion. It reminds us that what goes down must eventually come back up again, and that we aren't static beings; life is not a predictable wishy-washy soup of rinse-and-repeat cycles. It only takes one experience or chance encounter to turn our lives around.

Pay close attention, as opportunity is all about focus. Look for signs, chance meetings, or coincidences. They might have a much deeper meaning than you first think.

Reversed

Let go, let it flow. If things do not change, they can't improve. Are you resisting change out of fear of the unknown, or fear of the change itself?

Fabulous experiences are waiting for you. Holding on to situations, people, places, or even memories keeps you stuck in the past or just brings you more of the same, like reruns of a bad soap opera. Engage with change rather than blocking it.

JUSTICE

Karma, Legal Issues, Fairness, Balance

'The scales are tipping in your favour. Polish your sword of truth. Let harmony flow. Balance is restored.'

Justice can indicate contracts, legal issues, or simply doing the right thing. If something in your life requires fairness, this card implies that Justice will be done. However, it also urges us to fight for social justice and support the rights of others. When we challenge the injustice around us, we increase fairness for all.

Justice or injustice can be very subjective. We all view situations differently. We can sometimes feel like an injustice has been done, but we've got the wrong end of the stick. We can make assumptions and then dislike someone or feel insulted, hurt, slighted, or wronged, when that person means no harm or when the other person views the experience entirely differently. However, if you are waiting for an injustice to be resolved, this card is a positive one.

The Justice card reassures us that the outcome will be Universal Justice, where divine Karma is balanced – the Karma in which we all play a vital part.

Reversed

We may not be able to forgive someone. Sometimes, Justice asks us to hand our sense of injustice over to the Universe. We are not talking about forgiving the unforgivable, but for our own sake, knowing when to move on.

Justice's sword is two-edged and its scales finely balanced. I've also learned that sometimes Justice is not done in the moment, but that, in the end, Justice will be served. Be fair, be honest, and know that a proper resolution is on the way. Above all, don't be consumed with thoughts of retribution or revenge.

THE HANGED ONE

Limbo, Patience, Letting Go, Surrender

'Life is shaking a potent cocktail. Anticipate the pour. Drink the spirit of enlightenment slowly.'

Everything you seek will reveal itself in good time. You are walking in the magical in-between time, a place of potent power. Use this time to play, to do positive things that delight and inspire you. Point your energy in a new direction. Do you need to examine and heal your relationship to waiting? Does waiting feel like a rejection? Letting go of frustration and indulging in pleasurable experiences and creative activities can help speed things up, as can simply surrendering and accepting that the Universe has a plan.

When we look at the Hanged One, we see a meditative pose, one of surrender and handing over any desire to control to a deeper wisdom. You may feel like you have to sacrifice something to gain a deeper treasure. What you seek will come in the fullness of time or you will be released back into the flow of life again. Accept that the Cosmos has your back and that what's delivered may not be what you think you want, but is likely to be exactly what you need.

Reversed

Trying to force a situation will only create blocks and barriers to progress. Let go of any temptation to try to control or bring about a specific outcome, as all you will create is further frustration. Relax and examine where your frustration is coming from.

Stalk your thoughts and don't let fear take hold, as fear is what fuels the desire to force or control. Change is already in motion beneath the surface. Trust that.

DEATH

Endings, Rebirth, Transition

'Eternity is a kaleidoscope of changing scenes, each one a reimagining, never an ending.'

The great cycle of life insists that the old dies to make way for the new. The Death card doesn't usually mean literal death, but it does speak of endings – with rebirth to follow. You can't have a beginning of something without there having been an end of whatever came before it. You meet your ideal partner(s), and you end your life as a single person. You become a parent, and you not only have a new human being but a new life for yourself, too.

Death speaks of the need to clear out whatever is blocking the new growth in your life. One phase is ending as a new one waits to be born. Death arrives to remind us that everything has its season and then passes, but that new life always follows. We can look forward to the new as surely as we can mourn what's passing. It's time to clear out your past clutter, both physical and emotional, and make way for an incredible, fresh phase. It's a rebirth, and you are the phoenix rising.

Reversed

Are you resisting change? Hanging on to something that doesn't work delays the inevitable and creates blocks in our energy and progress. Sweet spirit, letting go of what no longer serves you will bring you many gifts. Release into the new.

Rebirth and reimagination await you if you surrender to a new path.

TEMPERANCE

Balance, Harmony, Tranquillity

'Shedding a skin of chaos balance brings us home, one foot on water, one on land. Wings outstretched we rise.'

Congratulations, Temperance is about to give you wings of peace and harmony. We rarely know that we're out of balance or the consequences of it at the time. However, when we get our flow back, we marvel at our ability not to see what is under our nose! Balancing our energy not only makes us feel better but also increases our ability to create our future and enjoy our present. It super-boosts our happiness and sense of well-being. Ask yourself how balanced you are right now. Do you have the space to sift through what's going on in your life and create solutions? If you have a problem with love or relationships, watch how things change when you regain balance. When we act out our insecurities, not only do we give our power away, we get further away from getting our needs met. Temperance isn't about self-denial but liberation. Be a warrior of love for your body, mind, and patterns. Address self-medication, energies, and habits that restrict your freedom and growth. You are powerful, and you've boldly and bravely come this far. Temperance urges us to celebrate and nurture ourselves. Is it time to empower yourself with fresh choices? Is it time to go directly to your needs and ask for what you need others to give you? Focus on what needs fine-tuning. When we get to a point where we have inner harmony, we can achieve anything we desire. In a way, it's akin to going through an initiation. You're upping your game, evolving your soul, and leveling up.

Reversed

What or who is creating imbalance in your life or blocking that divine flow? We all love to indulge in naughty pleasures but are you ignoring self-destructive patterns? Examine all your habits and daily routines and be honest with yourself about what you need to change. It's time for a realignment to your own authenticity. Inner balance brings about the same effect in your relationships – and the world around you.

THE DEVIL

Obsessions, Addictions, Excess, Chains

'Intoxicating beats strum on rhythms of our past. We unclasp ourselves from choices that shackle us to the pain, reclaiming our true power and stepping through to fresh domains.'

The Devil card talks to us about our addictions; they are our shadow-selves, which say 'yes' to people, obsessions, and desires that we know are destructive. To what or whom are you giving your power away? Look out for manipulative forces or temptations you know are unsuitable for you.

Power, control, domination, manipulation, and dependency may be undercurrents around you. Are you being made to feel you couldn't manage or cope without someone or something? Because if you're being made to feel powerless, it may be you, and not the other party, who has the power to change the dynamic. If you look at the card characters, you can see that they could take the chains from around their neck and break free at any time. Are you ready to escape?

Reversed

The time has come and you're ready to reconnect to your strength. The chains are falling as you finally release yourself from a situation or person that was oppressive. Seek out emotional or practical support to encourage you on this brave step forward. You take your power back. It was always yours. You see that clearly now.

THE TOWER

Shocks, Surprises, Revelations, Freedom

'Surprise eruptions knock out false foundations. Shocks shatter the peace, but what remains grows stronger.'

Don't panic when this card turns up. I'll be the first to admit that this is the card always accompanied by an 'oh no!' and a sharp intake of breath. Exhale, dear soul, because nothing can dim that vibrancy for long. Behind the drama lies your freedom. The Tower brings something crashing down or turfs us out of the ivory one we've been living in. It's a shocking – and often powerful – awakening that brings us down to earth with a crash of reality. But it may be needed: the outcome is awakening, freedom, and liberation, often from something we'd outgrown or which was going nowhere. So, what collapses may be necessary for our evolution and future happiness. Yes, the Tower often brings with it a shock or surprising twist in the tale. We are knocked off balance by something unexpected. Those carefully crafted plans collapse. You may feel utterly unprepared for it as it happens, so take all the time you need to process. But the aftermath can put you back on course if you've drifted off. You can head down paths you would never have taken otherwise. If you find yourself in an overwhelming situation or an unwelcome event, know that this too shall pass and that your life and soul path is about to be built on much firmer foundations.

Reversed

You're at a time of inner turmoil and transformation. Dramatic changes might be confusing, so it's important to express what you feel. Reversed, the Tower brings a surprise or setback – but not necessarily a disaster. It all depends on how we personally interact with change. Internalizing our fear, anger, or true feelings keeps us from moving forward.

Change is coming, so try to embrace rather than resist it – it could reveal itself to be a blessing in disguise.

THE STAR

Healing, Inspiration, Hope

'A new dawn after a spiritual storm washes doubt away. You are dazzled again, inspiration soaking through you as the stars dance in your DNA.'

The Star comes after the Tower, reconnecting us to faith and future promise. After destruction, collapse, and upheaval comes hope, healing, inspiration, and flow. The Star opens us to unconditional love and creativity, which pours through our spirit. In fact, Rider–Waite refers to this card as 'the gift of the spirits'. It's a time of connection, possibility, and restored faith in ourselves and possibly in life itself. Do you feel an awakening? The chaotic storm has come to an end, or perhaps it's the end of that long slog of mundane reality when you feel you are going nowhere! Suddenly you have an 'ah-ha!' moment; you're back in the game.

There's an air of magic and promise around you right now. Allow your soul to receive a much-needed reboot.

Reversed

It's time to reclaim your trust in the Universe. Have you given up or felt lost and alone? Does it seem as though there's no way out? Has someone stolen your dreams or an event caused you to give up hope? The Star is lighting up your spirit, but only you can nurture the sparks.

Take small steps towards healing. Imagine inspiration and creativity flowing through you. Possibilities and potential light your way like guiding stars as you steer the ship of your soul in a new direction of hope and future promise.

THE MOON   SPREAD OVER TWO CARDS

Mysteries, Secrets, Knowing

'Wild winds of intuition untangle lost feelings loosening, past passions. Fears float to the surface to be cleansed by the light of the Moon.'

Pay attention, wonderful one. The tide is rising along with your intuition. What is unconscious becomes conscious as feelings and deep knowing rise to the surface. Like the Moon, we all have our cycles. We can feel energized or need time alone. We can be highly intuitive and yet still sometimes feel disconnected to our inner wise one. This is why there are two cards representing the Moon in this deck. You can choose one to be a New Moon (letting go, making wishes, a new cycle) or Full Moon (a peak experience). Choose the one which best reflects your current phase – your intuition knows which one this is – or leave both cards in the deck. The decision is yours.

You're in a time of deep inner knowing. Listen to your inner voice. It has the answer to a current dilemma or question. Face the emotional truth and act on it. Be aware you're bathed in magic now. Look out for signposts and messages via dreams or strange coincidences that have a deeper meaning. Step into the intuitive magic which is always waiting to be accessed within you.

Reversed

Is there an uncomfortable intuition rising to the surface? Do you have a gut feeling that you're ignoring? If you feel doubt about a person or situation, don't ignore it. That persistent thought or feeling asks that you explore it further. You may not yet have the facts to back up those feelings, but time will tell just how accurate they are. Alternatively, emotional manipulation may be what's making you feel so uneasy. Is someone taking advantage of your caring, sensitive soul? Take protective measures with your energy if so.

THE SUN

Joy, Pleasure, Childlike Wonder

'Radiant with pleasure. Laughter our fuel. Flying a flag of hope. As we dance in the now.'

Step into life-affirming warmth and empowerment. Here comes the Sun. Feel unconditional love radiating in your heart and then outwards, connecting you to fierce, uncomplicated joy. You're about to sense the glee of being alive. Your inner child fills you with laughter and playfulness. If you had all the confidence in the world, what would you do? Where would you put your energy? The Sun ignites your fire, passion, and enthusiasm.

The Sun is the source of all life on our planet, so its appearance means that it's a great time to launch into anything you fancy doing. The Sun warms you and shares the wisdom that, through you allowing yourself to be happy, recharges you and, in turn, should you wish, gives you more energy to support and help others. You are finding out what makes your spirit soar, and making this a part of your soul journey.

Reversed

Are there emotional rain clouds in your tender heart?

Who or what has caused the rain to fall?

Dry your tears and turn your face back towards fun, creativity, and pleasure. It's time to nurture and play with your inner child. Find joy in the small things you love to do. Avoid and detox from negative people. Don't dismiss fun as superficial or non-spiritual. Fun is a necessary healing tonic, and your prescription from the Universe! Fear not – happiness is on the way.

JUDGEMENT

New Path, Revelations, Rebirth

'A revelation is coming that sets you free. Gallop towards the opening road.'

Awaken, soul warrior, and rise again. Liberation is coming. As the saying goes, 'The truth will set you free'. Have you had to deal with uncomfortable truths or a sudden revelation? You've arrived at a crossroads and, no matter what smoke and mirrors others cast before you, you now know the path you have to journey ahead.

When the truth is revealed, there's no going back. It's time to rise: rise to your magnificence, rise to your wisdom, and rise towards your chosen destiny. A situation you thought was over comes alive again. This is because there is still another chapter to be written. Your chrysalis is splitting and your butterfly wings, although still damp, are ready to surprise you with flight.

Reversed

Are you trying to keep something alive that needs to be surrendered? If so, it's time to release it with all the grace and acceptance contained within your magnificent spirit. You have the strength now.

Allow yourself to mourn if needed. Refusing to accept something is at an end only prolongs our pain. Let go and move on, so true healing can begin. The future is waiting.

THE WORLD

Blessings, Peaks, Completion

'Spinning through the cycles of life. A merry-go-round of cosmic alchemy through soft clouds. You reach its peak. Savour the view. Another chapter awaits.'

Congratulations, wondrous one! You are about to reach a peak experience and the next step in your personal evolution and growth! You're approaching a milestone, a reward, a time of 'all is well', and a cycle of completion. Celebrate the moment, breathe in your victory, and revel in your well-deserved arrival.

The World reminds us that life is all just a dance, and we should step lightly. We dance with the entire cycle of existence to different rhythms at different times, flowing with all of the energies that swirl around us. The World tells us that, while you might be at the end of one chapter, a whole book is waiting to be written. Prepare yourself for wonder as another journey begins.

Reversed

Has your World been turned upside down? Don't give up.

The World will always turn, and this too shall pass. Trust in your journey and where you're being led. The World reversed compels us to look at our problems and our life differently. Change your perspective and you literally change your World. Think of three people that inspire you and ask yourself: what advice would they give you? Dialogue with them in your imagination. Absorb their wisdom. How do they see things differently from you?

How does this change the way you view your situation? The outcome you seek might be cloaked in fog, but opportunity and solutions are there if you look for them. Be ready to reboot your journey.

MINOR ARCANA

WANDS
FIRE
ARIES, LEO, SAGITTARIUS

CUPS
WATER
CANCER, PISCES, SCORPIO

PENTACLES
EARTH
TAURUS, VIRGO, CAPRICORN

SWORDS
AIR
GEMINI, LIBRA, AQUARIUS

ACE OF WANDS

Feel the sparks rising and a rush of passion ignite your inner flame! The Ace of Wands is the peak experience of fire. Achievement, passion, and a lust for life ignite your potential. You are about to step into your power and the realization that you have the ability to achieve your goal.

You're a firebrand igniting a new cycle of possibility. Are you ready to grasp the magical baton and take up the challenge? There's a wanton fearlessness that this Ace brings, giving us the ability to make full use of our creativity and strength along with a fierce desire to achieve or experience the new. Your confidence soars. You can taste victory, which sends you racing down a new path.

The Ace of Wands fills you with courage and an overwhelming desire for adventure. You are bold, brazen, and free to create as you kick-start a creative project or journey.

Reversed

Are you stuck in inertia? Missing your mojo?

Lost your confidence, your self-belief, or even your sensuality? The Ace of Wands reversed can indicate a time of self-doubt and a bad case of the 'meh's. Think about ways you can reclaim your power. What small actions can you take to move forward? What single thought can you change to reframe your self-belief? One idea can turn into a catalyst for change if you let it. Plug back into self-empowerment.

TWO OF WANDS

Reflecting on your own cosmic Universe and where you're heading leads to a surprise revelation. The Two of Wands says to step out of the known and into a wider experience. It's time to let your visionary side out and plot your next move.

Experiment and play with your ideas. Initiate and instigate. If you've been cosmically sprouting plans, now is the time to act on them. Have faith in yourself, beautiful soul, and launch that vision skywards.

Oh, and an offer is coming your way, which might turn out to be far more significant or valuable than you first thought. Be open to acceptance. The spark of your future is contained within what you have right now, in the present.

Reversed

Don't just talk a good game – bring it.

The Two of Wands reversed speaks about all talk and no action, either by you or someone else. Act on those ideas. Follow through on the changes you say you're going to make. If someone doesn't keep their word or dishes out the silent treatment, take it as the end of the conversation and move on.

THREE OF WANDS

Ready to launch? You've reached a point where you want to broaden your horizons, plan an adventure, and sweep into a more abundant future. Ever since I first started reading Tarot as a small child, I always experienced this card as being related to the past, thinking about the past and looking backwards in order to reshape our future.

For the future to be different from our past, we need to stop making the same mistakes. You stand at a crossroads when the Three of Wands appears. Do you turn back towards what's familiar or take the road less traveled? Are you ready to choose change and step into a different destiny? If you decide to take that first step, the cosmos will help light your way.

Reversed

Are you letting the past control your future?

Time to let go of old patterns and decisions and to stop playing it too safe. To discover wonder, we have to leave behind the familiar. Connect to the explorer within. Rekindle the spirit of courage and dare to make a different choice this time around.

FOUR OF WANDS

Where we live is incredibly important as it's an extension of our soul. Each home we live in represents a different energy and lesson. The Four of Wands can usher in a new home, move, family celebration, or experience of living. Get ready for joy and pleasure connected to your surroundings and loved ones. You may feel compelled to redecorate, or someone could be moving in or moving out.

Our living space is our temple. Our retreat from the world where we nurture ourselves and recharge our batteries. Our place of safety. It's where we create our connections, memories, and our support structure. Prepare to celebrate a new cycle or lifestyle choice. A party or get-together could offer something more intriguing or beneficial than expected.

Reversed

Check the energy around your living arrangements.

Does it feel stale, stagnant, stuck or 'lived out'? Is your space stuffed with clutter? Have you simply outgrown it? Or has it ceased to be the safe haven for you that it once was? Reversed, the Four of Wands tells you it's time to move on in some way and that a change of energy is needed. Sometimes this can be as simple as rearranging our space and getting rid of what we no longer use or need.

Other times it calls for an actual physical move away from our current residence or living situation. It may be time to uproot yourself on some level and put down new ones someplace else.

FIVE OF WANDS

The Five of Wands shows what happens when our energy gets scattered, when too many small, snarky problems are allowed to interrupt our flow, or when we get caught in a loop of bickering with ourselves or others for the sake of it.

The five figures in this card could achieve so much more if they aligned their energy or banded together to achieve a single goal. Together they could rule the world – or at least triumph. Instead, none of them are on the same page. This card tells you to adopt a 'first things first' approach to getting things done and to look very carefully at where your time and focus goes.

It's time to get more organized. Reclaim your purpose and channel your power back into that outcome. Weed out distractions that divert you from what you want to achieve.

Reversed

Are you running around putting out other people's fires, not because you want to help them, but because this stops you from having to look at what needs fixing in your own life?

Courageous soul, you are braver than you think! Ditch the distraction. Awaken your inner visionary. The Five of Wands reversed says get your act together and fix the problem once and for all.

SIX OF WANDS

Hooray!

You're conquering a situation, achieving an ambition, and being seen for who you are. On top of that, you believe in yourself.

When we think we can accomplish a goal and that we deserve it, we open a magical portal to success. Okay, we also have to do the hard graft, but this card shouts out, 'It's worth it!'

The image of the woman on this card was taken from an image of a Suffragette riding jubilantly for her rights at a women's suffrage rally. Often victory occurs after a sustained, soul-testing effort. The Six of Wands indicates that you'll have a fabulous moment of triumph and well-deserved praise. Don't rest on your laurels, though, a whole new challenge awaits.

Reversed

Have you lost your belief in just how glorious you are? Reversed, the Six of Wands whispers of a lost opportunity to shine or make your mark. Was it self-doubt that held you back?

Fear of failure? Or even fear of success? Examine without judgement or self-blame why you may have let something slip through your fingers. Sometimes we ensure we can't fail simply by not trying at all.

But that also means we can't succeed either. There's so much within you that you have yet to access and discover. You are far more capable than you believe. Recapture this truth for when opportunity returns with another offer for you.

SEVEN OF WANDS

Connect to what you know is right and stand your ground!

Right now, you might feel like you're under intense pressure from all sides. But this card tells you not to give up as the battle is nearly over.

Don't let anyone influence your stance if it means compromising or selling out. This card tells you that your position is secure and that the conflict will shortly come to an end. You're on top, you're winning!

Sometimes we just have to take a stand and tough it out. Especially if this means standing for what we believe in or no longer being willing to pretend to be anything other than who we are anymore. Let others know where you draw the line.

Reversed

If you stand for nothing, you fall for anything – or anyone for that matter.

The Seven of Wands reversed is telling you to reconnect to your core strength of belief and not to go along with something you don't believe in just to conform, people-please, or keep the peace.

Let others know what you stand for and speak in your authentic voice. Those who think the same way will find you. Your people are out there.

EIGHT OF WANDS

In the original Rider–Waite–Smith deck, this card was called the Arrows of Love. A surge of activity sends your life into fast-forward.

However, as the Cosmos is the wind beneath your wings, it's likely to be a pleasure ride. Lucky breaks, career opportunities, solutions, opportunities, and even love sweep you up, up, and away. They take you higher, faster, than you ever imagined possible.

It's love and life lived at the speed of light now, as exciting events, news, and slews of messages, meetings, emails, and even people appear, capture your imagination and your heart, and fling you along with their momentum.

Travel may also feature since this card is also associated with flight, arrivals, and departures. Writing, communication, publishing, and the internet are your hunting grounds and your manifesting catalogue. Get ready to leave the mundane behind.

Reversed

Are you clinging to that comfort zone? It's time to reawaken your fighting spirit and desire to experience the new.

Like the hero (or, as I like to say, her-o!) in the Hero's Journey, you may initially resist the call to adventure. But then the Universe steps in and calls again.

And this time, you answer. Ready yourself, tender spirit. You're not forgotten.

The call will come again.

NINE OF WANDS

Constantly on the alert, the figure shields themselves behind a barrier of their own making, staring fearfully into the distance. What caused them to be constantly on the defensive?

Perhaps you too have had to put up an emotional shield, retreating behind your armour of safety after suffering repeated disappointments and energetic blows? Or perhaps you've fought a battle on behalf of others but which you knew was the right thing to do?

Whether you've faced inner or outer conflict, you now feel exhausted and have had to become a God(dess/dex) of self-protection, waiting for the next battle to appear. Your strength cannot be underestimated. And your wounds and ability to survive tell you that there's nothing you cannot overcome. Is it time to drop your defences? Are you cutting yourself off from life and others because of your past? Or is that sensitivity that you've had to hide in order to survive, causing you to overreact to what is happening in the present?

Know that in what you see as your vulnerability lies your strength. Plan for a future where you can let down your guard and dance with life again. You are safe. You are free.

Reversed

Has someone taken advantage of your deep well of tenderness, your generosity of spirit, and ability to care?

More to the point, have you continued to let them? Maybe you've told yourself it's no biggie and doesn't matter, or you've selflessly given your time, love, or other resources only to discover they weren't there for you when you needed them. Small things mount up when we're dealing with energy vampires or those who constantly ask for favours but give nothing in return. The Nine of Wands reversed speaks of a lack of boundaries and tells you that you need to lay firm ones now. It may be all you need to do is say 'no' to take your power back.

TEN OF WANDS

Your goal is almost in sight – but make sure you haven't taken on too much and watch for burnout. If you look at the way the wands are being carried, it's not the most practical!

You may need to shed some of your responsibilities, to delegate, or simply streamline your focus. Ten is the number of completion, of bringing something to a close with a fresh start or rebirth to follow. Often this means shedding part of our load to reach that finish line. Look at what you no longer need to carry with you in order to get what you want.

The Cosmos is telling you 'good job' for seeing this through to the end. Be ready to accept victory. Be proactive and objectively look at what you can delegate and pass on to others to deal with. Relinquish your old coping mechanisms to free yourself to follow the new path that's opening up for you.

Reversed

Are you being expected to take on more than humanly possible? Check your ability to say 'no'. But if you're being offered more responsibility that comes with equal rewards, don't shy away from the task ahead.

This card says that you're more capable than you know. That said, don't automatically assume others are too. Someone may be struggling and putting on a brave face.

If that's you – time to own it and ask for help. You may feel you have to be superhuman. But even superstars need backup.

ACE OF CUPS

The Ace of Cups brings with it an outpouring of positive emotion – it's the mystical grail of pleasure.

You're being offered a divine chalice, overflowing with joy and possibility. Love – a peak emotional experience – oneness with life, and a sense of gratitude abound. Abundance flows effortlessly.

Drink from the goblet of life. Quench your desire with the outflow of passion surrounding you. Feel the unconditional love of the Universe enter you.

Creativity and inspiration are rippling out from the divine source. The appearance of the Ace of Cups often brings in a new relationship or cycle of relating. You draw love to you in all its many forms. But you want to give as much as you are open to receiving, and others are drawn to that tender beating heart you're wearing on your sleeve. Trust your feelings and go where your heart wants to take you now.

Reversed

The promise is broken. The potential remains unrealized. Guard against putting a lover or friend on a pedestal. Has the cup of love been kicked over? Your intuition picks up on others' potential, but you need to make sure it isn't fantasy.

Take your time with relationships if you want to avoid disappointment further down the road. Look closely at any patterns in your history or the other party's. Reversed, this card tells you that you have an opportunity to finally step free of a negative emotional cycle that has kept you trapped.

Know what the deal breakers are in any relationship and stick to them.

TWO OF CUPS

Two energies, minds, and hearts meet as one. The perfect duo, double act, or soul connection. There's no hidden agenda when we are in a Two of Cups relationship.

When the Two of Cups alights in our reading, we're looking at the perfect balancing act between us and another soul, a real and equal union which asks for nothing in return. Whether this is a love affair, a friendship, or the coming together of two people for a job, purpose, or project, just being in each other's company ignites a strange kind of magic. It makes both parties feel good and reach for the best possible version of themselves.

These enchanted connections are extremely rare and are usually Karmic in nature. This is a soul connection that brings the divine gift of mutual healing.

Communication is free-flowing and easy. When we meet a spiritual being that 'gets' us, it empowers our journey. And we do the same for them. Love comes in many forms, so be open to the one this connection takes.

Align with those who have your best interests in mind. Open your heart to new people. Rekindle and appreciate the love already around you. Know that you are loved and that love will find you. It is time.

Reversed

The Two of Cups is a beautiful card all about love, equality, and those who mirror our souls. Are you still waiting for them to appear? Do you believe that this kind of love exists? Or have past disappointments replaced love with cynicism? Time to heal the wounds if so.

The Two of Cups reversed can also remind us to look at what brought us together in the first place. Focus on what we share rather than the natural differences that form part of the package of being two individuals. If there's been a shift around your connection lately, it tells you that recapturing the magic is still possible.

THREE OF CUPS

Rejoice in friendship! You have something to share and celebrate.

Two's company but three's a party with the Three of Cups as you enjoy the pleasure of like-minded souls. Invitations and good times make memories that cement your ties to others. Pamela Colman-Smith, who created the original image for this card, was a part of the Suffragette movement and understood the power of shared beliefs and how they can not only change our lives but the lives of others.

Join in. Find your people. Connect. It's doesn't matter if your intention is a project or simply play, a political movement or a celebration. It's about the group experience and being uplifted by it.

'Life is a party and everyone's invited' is the message behind this card. When we join with others whose vibration matches our own, we create a force field of intention which sets in motion events greater than the sum of their parts.

Reversed

Are you hanging out with the wrong crowd, bending yourself out of shape and trying to fit in or impress the wrong people? A friendship may not be what you think, or you may suddenly find yourself an outlier instead of at the centre of your usual circle.

That resonance you once felt for a friend or even a group is missing. If so, the Three of Cups reversed says it's time to move on.

FOUR OF CUPS

I'll let you in on a mind-blowing secret.

We have UNLIMITED choices. It's an illusion to think there are only one or two answers or options, no matter what our situation. Past conditioning along with the rigidity of life and the patriarchy limit our perceptions. Also, most of us are hardwired to want to try to control the outcomes we want and hold tight to the reins of our destiny. But in doing so, we avoid something better.

The Four of Cups is telling you that there's another option or alternative available to you that you cannot see. This may be because you are so focused on one specific result that you're unaware of other possibilities or that something better may even exist. So, open your psychic senses and connect to your intuition to discover how much more could be waiting for you.

Shift your focus and let abundant choice flow.

Reversed

Avoid being so certain something better will be on offer that you let a golden opportunity slip through your fingers. Or putting off RSVPing to the last moment in case a more interesting alternative turns up...

Only one doesn't and it's now too late to accept the first, so you end up drinking wine/kombucha and boxset-bingeing by yourself instead. If you're living life without making plans, life will make plans without you. Start saying 'yes' and stick to that whether something 'better' turns up or not. Life wants you to experience the best it has to offer.

FIVE OF CUPS

Who kicked my cups over? When we experience disappointment, it's only natural that we focus on that. Our hearts hurt. Our expectations are crushed, our dreams fallen. Or so it seems. Like the figure in this card, we don't see the fact that two brimming cups remain upright.

The Five of Cups promises that all is not lost. The two cups that survive contain more future potential than we can ever imagine. Their wonders and magic are available; we just need to turn around and see them. Know you can move away and soar!

Be patient, sweet soul. You may be unaware that your process of transformation has already begun. But soon your focus will shift away from what is lost or spilled to what was always waiting there for you.

The change within you sees you ready to unfurl your spirit wings of shining future potential. You grab the two remaining cups and fly towards a brand-new beginning.

Reversed

You need gentle healing now and the gift of self-acceptance. Know you're entitled to feel what you feel, no matter your circumstances. There is no statute of limitations on our emotions.

It's natural to mourn, whether the loss is a relationship, job, friendship, or cycle of life. But if we try to take refuge in denial or hang on to false hope, we can't move forward. You have two avenues to explore or people to turn to now.

Your intuition guides you to the right healing choices to make.

SIX OF CUPS

Travel back in time and experience a return to innocence.

The meaning of the Six of Cups is both sacred and profound. It signifies a past life connection or simply a connection to our past in this one, a tie to a pure-hearted love, infused with childlike innocence.

It shows us that we are all connected – across time, space, the miracle of the multiverse, and across many lifetimes too.

If someone new enters your life, it may seem like you've known them for ever. Something from your past may return now, or you may even travel back to places that contain happy memories or, even if this is your first visit, that feel oddly familiar. Soul contracts are honored. Good Karma gets paid forward. This card tells you to expect a sign or proof that love is eternal.

Reversed

Gentle heart! Don't let others dim your childlike sense of wonder and belief in the power of love.

Trust that you have more resources within you than you know, and all ready to be awakened. Above all, don't think that love has passed you by. Despite being reversed, this card promises that other soul connections will pop into your life just when you least expect it. You are infinitely connected to a divine source.

Whatever you're waiting for, a loving energy is coming to help or just to remind you of the magic that exists in the Cosmos. While you wait, surround yourself with people that get you: old pals, spiritual connections, and pure spirits. Your journey back to love has begun.

SEVEN OF CUPS

Many choices hang before you like a tantalizing and magical wish list.

However, it's up to you – you need to take action to make them real. You're faced with a vast web of possibility. It might not feel like it, but choices need to be made.

The thing with options is that, although we feel like we have free will, we are often ruled by our unconscious and by past patterns.

The joyful message of the Seven of Cups is that, if we choose wisely or boldly, we can unearth fresh experiences, happiness, and fulfilment. Avoid choosing the painful experiences of the past. Thinking about an ex? Are they the snake or the rainbow? Use your intuition, gut feeling, and inner wisdom to go forwards.

Reversed

The time has come to stop fearing making the wrong choices. That, too, is a choice, but not one which gets you what you need. Don't let anyone pressure you to make a decision you know deep down is wrong for you.

You're worth more than that. Above all, avoid choosing the painful experiences of your past. Why would anyone do that? Because it feels familiar.

Exercise your right to pick your path with pure spiritual intent and your divine power. The Seven of Cups reversed says it's your choice. And you now have the choice to choose again.

EIGHT OF CUPS

Are you ready to go on a quest? This card whispers that it's time to find the missing piece. It's not about walking away from something bad necessarily, rather it's the story of a brave soul who seeks what's missing.

You may have many things in your life which are fabulous but your heart knows there's another adventure waiting for you. Having succeeded in some ways, your soul is craving the next challenge. If there's a situation in your life which isn't quite right, you've reached a time where you're ready to let go and hunt for what you truly desire. One word of caution – make sure you aren't leaving behind what you love just to continue to achieve for achievement's sake. Inner peace comes from within, not from superficial success. It's time to look for a life that truly reflects who we are. And in doing so, you may have to abandon something to discover what that looks like. Is this one of those times? You're seeking the missing piece, the Holy Grail of Love and True Purpose, the chalice of happiness. What is it that you truly want? What do you have to let go of to find it?

It can be as simple as an idea, a belief system, or as complex as a path or a person. You already know what it is. And you already know the first steps you need to take on your quest. Are you brave enough to enter the unknown? Yes! Don't look back.

Reversed

It's good to revisit the past. But you need to remember that you no longer live there. You're so focused on what might have been or 'the way we were' you might not be moving forward – which is what the Universe is asking you to do now. Let go of painful memories and even nostalgia.

Are you constantly reliving your victories, your glory days? Is it because, deep down, you don't believe your future can hold anything better? Write a love letter to your past thanking it for all the experiences it gave you. But then tell it you're ready to move on and find new ones now.

NINE OF CUPS

Wishes are granted and desires fulfilled. Fabulous news is on the way, with the possibility of more to come.

The most basic interpretation of the Nine of Cups is that you're being given a massive cosmic 'yes!' and heads-up that a wish is coming true. It's not the size of the wish but the manifestation that matters. It could be a large, long cherished one or a teeny-tiny minor one.

But it's a sign that you can harness the magic of manifestation and be the alchemist in your life, turning dreams into reality.

So why stop there? What wishes can you cast out to the Universe next? What reality would you like to conjure? What new magic can you create? When a desire is granted, it refuels our belief that anything is possible and reaffirms our power. Now you see the results, give thanks.

And give another wish a fresh set of wings.

Reversed

Perhaps your wish was granted, only for you to find you no longer wanted it.

Have those dreams and goals evolved along with you? Don't even attempt to manifest something you can no longer infuse with the genuine desire of passion. Reversed, the Nine of Cups is asking whether you need a new star to wish on?

Or do you believe you can never have what you want, no matter how hard you try, so you've simply stopped casting out your desires to the Universe? Wish fulfilment begins within us. We rekindle the magic of knowing we deserve good things.

If others see their dreams fulfilled and wishes granted, then why not us? Ask whether, deep down, you feel as if you don't deserve to be happy. Magic isn't something that happens to others. Make a wish to change that.

TEN OF CUPS

Experience divine connectivity. All the strands of the love you've put into the Cosmos are woven into a brilliant tapestry.

Your boundless compassion and ability to overcome hardships with your heart intact draws the perfect spiritual team to you. Over the coming days and weeks, you will know who your beloveds are: the ones that uplift your spirit and make your heart soar.

Those around us constantly impact our energy. Who we join forces with will ultimately enhance or hinder our dreams, our goals, and our ability to realize our true magnificence. You're about to experience an outpouring of love, relief, and gratitude as others uplift, connect, and work with you for your highest good.

A celebration is coming.

Reversed

If you don't feel like you've met your soul team yet or you've been disappointed by those you felt were 'family', open your arms to new possibilities. Seek and you shall find, as, even reversed, the Ten of Cups shows you that they await your arrival. Shake up that routine and venture forth in search of them.

Go to new places, explore, join in, and seek out groups where fellow love warriors are to be found. Ensure that they can find you in turn.

Either way, empowering, heart-centred connections are on the horizon.

ACE OF SWORDS

You are holding the essence of air in your hands. Your mind is rapier-sharp and filled with intention. You see everything clearly, cutting to the chase, getting things done, taking the action you need to gallop towards victory.

You may have to cast a cloak over your natural empathy and make a tough choice. Wield your sword kindly, though, with the impeccable truth of your heart.

Mind games and manipulation no longer work on you. You see right through any agenda. You are no longer willing to allow others to take advantage.

The Ace of Swords signifies intellectual strength, truth, and the peak of air energy. You will excel at pitching, strategic thinking, research, getting your ideas across, and going straight to the heart of the matter to get to the facts. Self-doubt and fears no longer stand in your way. Oh, and there's a possible increase in abundance.

Reversed

Don't allow yourself to become distracted or your truth to be shaken. And don't be made to doubt your inner resolve. You may be called on to stand by or defend your ideas or a principle.

How strong is your belief? But fear not. You are more than capable of meeting this challenge with your finely forged intellect and fierce heart.

The only way you can be overcome now is if you waver or allow self-doubt to cloud your vision. Stay true to it and have a strategy in mind which pierces through any obstacles you encounter.

TWO

SWORDS

TWO OF SWORDS

This card is one that I always think of as a 'double-edged sword'. You may feel frozen by indecision. Perhaps you're blocking your own intuition or know what action you need to take but ignore the answer because it will create temporary disruption?

The Two of Swords whispers you must trust your instincts. Perhaps you are so busy intellectualizing or overthinking the problem that you can't make a choice? Or maybe you feel that neither is quite right? Be at peace if you're truly unsure of what to do; the other edge of the sword is patience.

Ignore any pressure to take action in the moment, whether this comes from others or within. The Two of Swords is asking you whether you have to answer the question now. What is to be gained by deciding in this moment? Wait for your mind and heart to clear and connect to your centre. Time will provide clarity and show you which direction to take.

Reversed

If you need to act quickly but remain unsure of exactly what choice to make, there's a magical technique that you could try which involves holding two identically sized stones (or other objects). Decide which stone represents Choice 1 and Choice 2.

Before you pick up the stones, close your eyes and ask your question or for guidance as to which decision serves your greatest good right now.

Pick up the stones, remembering the choice each stone represents. Then .... take your time. Sit with the choices. Open yourself up to wisdom and higher truth. Finally, with your eyes still closed, feel which stone now feels heavier.

This may enable your intuition, your mind, and your heart to connect and deliver you the enlightenment you seek.

THREE OF SWORDS

The Three of Swords talks to us about buried pain. Most of us carry this with us, especially so if we've encountered more than our fair share of heartbreak or survived a traumatic experience. Our subconscious is excellent at hiding the wounds that run deep and refuse to heal.

We are all, in our essence, beacons of love. Old wounds, like scars, can feel so familiar that we become numb to their presence. But we still carry them. Even if we become super good at juggling our emotions, sooner or later, they surface. Isn't it better to rip off that psychic Band-Aid and allow the wound to finally heal so we can be free? The first step is admitting we're still carrying it and still in pain.

See the Three of Swords not as a reminder of a painful past, but as your key to escaping it. It tells you that you're ready for recovery, to experience abundance and joy. Your faith in your future is the final healing measure once you realize your past doesn't dictate how you can live, create, or experience it.

One of my mantras is: 'We are not out past, we are our future.'

You're ready now.

Reversed

You may be trying to do too much or be juggling conflicting priorities. Reversed, the Three of Swords tells us that one slip will result not just in being unable to keep those knives in the air, but that, if we drop one, we may injure ourselves in the process.

Someone or a situation may be creating an emotional conflict within. Your soul demands that you come from a place of honesty and integrity.

Time to do what you know is right and tackle this once and for all before your subconscious causes a slip-up that will force you to deal with it anyway.

FOUR OF SWORDS

Sweet soul, the Four of Swords talks of a time to rest, to chill out, and to focus on extreme self-care. It may be you've had to face challenges, reversals, illness, grief, or loss. Or that you've simply been running on empty. Are you emotionally, mentally, or spiritually exhausted?

Now is a moment to recover. You are as important, precious, and sacred as anyone else. Honor it now.

Perhaps you've had to remain strong for others and have been neglecting yourself? Time to press the reset button. Understand that you first need to be there for yourself in order to be there for others. Give your own well-being the priority it deserves. Allow the healing process to begin by taking care of yourself through resting, supporting, and nurturing your precious self.

Reversed

You are powerful and capable. But your resources are not infinite. Have you been showing the warning signs of stress or depletion lately? You know the symptoms. You start making mistakes. Your appetite and/or sleep patterns change. You lack energy or feel depressed. You begin to have out-of-character emotional outbursts over not very much at all. You forget things.

Get in front of this while you can. Self-priority asks for bravery and resetting your values to include the most important one of all: I matter.

FIVE OF SWORDS

Has someone stolen your swords?

Have you felt ripped off or treated badly? It can be hard to walk away from people or situations that hurt us. The Five of Swords suggests that what you've been dealing with is not only unfair but extreme.

Perhaps someone has overreacted or been too vengeful. If so, reflect on what caused that severe reaction. Does it come from vulnerability? Fear? Or not feeling good enough? Set firm boundaries with people who have anger issues, while also understanding your own relationship to anger.

When we dig beneath intense emotions, we find the key to our further healing.

Reversed

You can be on a fast track to success, but sometimes not everyone will be happy about that. Guard your ideas as others may try to take the credit. The fact you have the courage to follow your vision may have attracted jealousy or sparked insecurity in others.

Ensure you keep your goals close or only share them with folks you are certain will cheer you on. Our plans can be like the fragile souls of small children: they need protection and nurturing until they can walk on their own.

Keep the faith within until yours grow wings.

SIX OF SWORDS

You're in transition and at the start of an important journey.

It's a move away from choppy times into peaceful waters. Most of all, it's a period of emotional passage. You may not have wanted to move away from the safety of what you knew but felt you had no choice. Circumstances are cutting you free. No matter how it began, your courageous spirit acts as your inner navigator, steering you in a fresh direction. Well done!

You've jumped aboard and are committed to healing.

Before you arrive at your destination, it's important to deal with that excess baggage you may be carrying. Symbolically, this card asks that you leave all this behind you by the time you reach the other side. But if you take the swords out of the boat before you've fully healed, the boat might sink. Do the work. Be ready. The mysterious land of your future lies ahead.

Reversed

It's time to strive towards happiness and fulfilment. Instead of looking towards that horizon, are you still looking back to the land of regret and lost memories?

The ship of your soul is stuck in the shallows. But your spirit can set the voyage in motion again at any moment, like a breath of wind filling your sails. You deserve a future drenched in wonder, magic, and healing.

Jump aboard the boat of emotional passage and head to dry land.

SEVEN OF SWORDS

Intuition may be telling you that the person you believe has your back actually doesn't, or that someone may have a hidden agenda or simply doesn't deserve your trust.

People who throw shade disguised as caring, passive-aggressive behaviour, lost souls who enjoy creating conflict, energy vampires, and one-sided friendships are the obvious candidates for this card. As are liars. These folks are usually repeat offenders; don't indulge them.

Our intuition always acts as an early warning system telling us something is 'off' or that someone's energy doesn't feel right. No matter how charming they are, don't let them take advantage of you. This card warns you that appearances can be deceiving. Trust your gut and cast out anyone dodgy.

Reversed

Just because others resort to nasty, devious, and underhand tactics doesn't mean you should sink to their level.

Reversed, the Seven of Swords tells you to hang tight to your integrity. Don't get dragged into game playing or the desire for petty revenge.

Is this a repeat offender? Reach for a new set of tools and integrity rules to deal with them. Above all, don't give them what they want, which is for you to lose your cool. You don't have to have the last word. Sometimes simply disengaging is all you need to do.

Yes, someone may have crossed the line or committed a big betrayal. Your anger may be justified. There may also be no excuses for their behaviour. But vengeance comes at a cost, and if you overreact, all that usually happens is that you end up being cast as the 'bad' one instead. However, this doesn't mean you can't seek justice.

Protect yourself and your heart by not giving in. Love yourself enough to walk away.

EIGHT OF SWORDS

Imprisoned by their thoughts, the figure in the Eight of Swords has no idea they are free to escape at any time. What's the idea that's keeping you stuck? Are you so focused on the problem that you can't see the solution that's right in front of you?

When we're faced with challenges or testing times, emotional pain can blindfold us to the alternatives at our feet. Worries, emotional storms, and negativity steal our perspective, and in the end that is all we can see. We become blind to the truth of our situation.

Know that you are no longer a prisoner to whatever it is that's preventing you from moving forward again. Despite what you may believe, solutions are at hand. When you look back at this period, you will see so clearly that the way forward for you was obvious all along.

Reversed

Are you hiding from the truth? Your intuition is telling you it is time to face facts. Don't shove it aside or ignore it. If someone points out the reality of your situation to you, avoid reacting defensively.

Reversed, the Eight of Swords says that, deep down, you're acutely aware of the reality which surrounds you but don't yet feel ready to face it. The truth will set you free.

NINE OF SWORDS

Worries, fears, and pressure can cause restless and sleepless nights. Perhaps you're feeling down or suffering from overthinking? Give yourself a break, stop blaming yourself, and pour yourself a good dose of self-love.

The figure in the card is caught in a twilight world where they cannot escape from their problems – problems which may now be magnified out of proportion.

Sweet soul, awaken. I'm not saying this is all a bad dream. Emotional pain is all too real. But know you don't have to endure this alone. You need the gift of another's point of view to restore your perspective and faith in the future.

Seek them out now: a friend, partner, or professional guide who has the compassion and life wisdom you need.

Awaken to a new day of hope.

Reversed

You are a spirit who cannot be defeated or crushed, and you have just proved that. Yes, your inner strength has been tested – possibly to its limits.

But your soul has been forged in the fires of transformation. You have overcome your problem and the situation is now turning around.

Sure, you may not have done this entirely on your own. Perhaps you've had to reach out and ask for help or admit that you were vulnerable, lost, or stuck. But true courage is knowing when we need to admit we can't do this alone.

TEN OF SWORDS

Most people see Ten of Swords as one of the 'worst' cards in the Tarot. After all, the figure has been stabbed in the back. But is there more to it than what we have been led to believe?

It can seem extremely difficult at first glance to discover the upside of this card but it does have one, and an important one. Yes, the Ten of Swords tells a story of broken promises, wrecked dreams, and betrayals. The uneasy feeling we had about someone in the Seven of Swords is now being inescapably confirmed. But look again. Behind the wounded figure, a constellation of stars sparkles in the sky. Glimmering with hope. Your illusions about someone may have been destroyed, but this frees you of illusions and makes way for beautiful connections.

Yes, it hurts when people we invest in let us down, but we all have a phoenix curled up in our DNA which will rise out of adversity, empowered and clear, reaching towards real, not fake, relationships.

Reversed

You know that friendship or group is actually deeply fake – the one that revolves around gossiping, plotting, or disrespecting other people. And you also know that's how they might talk about you when you're not present. Reversed, the Ten of Swords says, knowing this, isn't it time you separated yourself from them?

Time to make a strategic withdrawal. Master magicians and weavers of dreams deserve better.

Sometimes this card reversed forewarns us of a gathering storm in the form of a situation that's coming to an end, and gives us time to prepare or take action to avoid it entirely. Like that hunch or rumour that your job may be under threat, for instance. Knowledge is power. This card tells you to gather those vast resources of love within, and act with self-protection, respect, and integrity.

You know exactly what you need to do.

ACE OF PENTACLES

The height of earth energy, a diamond thought or possibility enriches your life. You've been inching towards building your self-esteem and healing past wounds, and it's now time to take care of the details. Know that you deserve success and that you've earned it, and that success is coming.

Influencers, powerful souls, and wise ones are all drawn to you. Commit to your dreams. Fight any fears or self-doubt. You've come this far and the next stage will likely feel simpler. The Ace of Pentacles assures you that you can and will do it. Ground yourself, look after yourself, and plant your seeds deeply. An abundance spurt it on the way!

It can usher in a renewed value in yourself and a greater appreciation for all you have accomplished. Because you now experience the results of what you can do, the prizes are more than money can buy. The Ace of Pentacles allows your self-worth and belief in your abilities to soar. You've done the real work and dug damn fine foundations for your future. It's time now to reap the rewards. Your time of abundance approaches!

Reversed

The Ace of Pentacles reversed says that your rewards are delayed as there is still work to be done. Go the distance now. The Cosmos is reminding you to stay grounded and maintain your focus.

Go back over your progress so far. This should show you just how far you have come. But is there something you have overlooked or room for improvement?

It's time to reinvest in that focus, idea, or vision. Victory is so close you can probably almost taste it. Believe in your power to triumph. One final push brings you the result you've worked so hard to achieve.

TWO OF PENTACLES

Look closely at the pentacles in this card and you'll see the symbol of infinity surround them.

This card reminds us that we're constantly surrounded by flow and unlimited abundance. But there's a second message with this card, too, and that's of partnership. It tells us nobody does it alone. If you have a product or service, you need customers or visitors. Even if your job involves flying solo – say you are a writer or musician – you still need a publisher, agent, or an audience for your work.

Who do you need to partner with to increase the flow in your life? What do you need to create or send out there to engage with the infinite cycle of abundance? Sometimes all we need to do is partner with ourselves to open up to it.

The universal current flows your way.

Reversed

Are your resources stretched too thin?

When the Two of Pentacles is reversed, we can also see money flowing down the drain. We may feel time poor as well as financially strapped.

You may discover that you and someone else don't share the same values or that you may have very different attitudes to how you deal with your cash. Look to whether something is worth the continued investment.

This can be anything from an idea to a connection. A whole life budget may be necessary. Direct your precious resources – especially your creativity and love – to where they are best invested now.

THREE OF PENTACLES

Reach for confidence and self-belief, and don't be afraid to be a self-starter now.

Own your talents, skills, and abilities. The Three of Pentacles has you showing the world all you have to offer.

You're willing to put yourself out there and to display your wares, ideas, and visionary uniqueness. Whatever makes you stand out, the Three of Pentacles is all about laying firm foundations so that what you build is solid and secure.

When this card turns up, it tells you it's time. Time to apply for that job, start that course or apprenticeship, submit that manuscript, pitch that project, launch that plan, or set your ideas free to take flight.

Resist any desire to remain behind the scenes. Your unique vibrancy is also your unique selling point! Why keep it under wraps? You deserve to be recognized and to shine. Share all you have to offer and don't doubt for a moment that you have what it takes to succeed.

Reversed

Are you feeling overlooked or unappreciated at work?

Reversed, the Three of Pentacles says you aren't receiving the recognition or rewards you deserve, or that your current position simply doesn't offer the satisfaction and stimulation that you need.

Begin by honestly asking whether what you're doing or where you do it is really right for you. If it's not, what actions do you need to take to begin to set positive change in motion?

Whether your work is paid or unpaid, infuse it with purpose again and see it as a platform which provides you with shining satisfaction and rewards.

FOUR OF PENTACLES

Sweet soul, have you been feeling the need to protect yourself?

While it's right and powerful to withdraw occasionally, make sure that you aren't blocking yourself from positive experiences. When we feel hurt or mistreated, it can hinder our ability to trust. Whatever you do, don't block the flow now! Don't allow self-sabotage, self-doubt, or feelings of unworthiness to cut you off from the abundance that's trying to reach you. This can be a card of holding on tight, though not out of love, but out of fear. What are you fearful of losing? Sometimes this can even be a fear of taking a chance because we don't think we deserve anything better than what we currently have. Don't cling to the status quo – open your mind to new possibilities for yourself. Understand abundance is infinite and so are the opportunities that are available to you. You're urged to examine how well shutting down is working for you. Is it time to open up your heart again? The winds of wonder want to blow through you; the magic of life wants to be available to you. We've all been in those terrible times when we build a wall to protect ourselves. But when we do block ourselves, we stop our energy moving. In effect, we imprison ourselves in the wound. It may be time to heal now and taste freedom again. It may be time to let your spirit do a little jig and get back on your soul path. My advice? Believe in possibility again – you deserve it!

Reversed

There's a need for soul conservation when the Four of Pentacles is reversed.

Are you being too generous, for instance? Do those you shower with your abundant generosity appreciate it and do the same in return?

This reversal warns of scattering your resources or simply the need to take a more mindful and caring approach to valuing what you have – and that includes yourself. You are your own most precious resource. Your love, especially, is too important to give away to those who don't understand the treasure they have.

FIVE OF PENTACLES

This card speaks of being 'left out in the cold'.

Times may have been tough for you recently. Money may have been hard to come by, but this card also speaks of emotional poverty.

You can weather this storm. Within you, hope and inner resolve still burn bright. This too shall pass. But, for the time being, you need and deserve compassion and to know your feelings count.

If you look at the card, you can see that sanctuary is right there but the characters in the card can't quite see what is in front of them. The Five of Pentacles shows us that the divine light of warmth and hope still shines on us and is waiting for us to turn around and notice this. Help is at hand – but you have to seek it out. Have you become so used to this emotional state or struggle that it's become your new normal and you're now stuck in it? Try making even the smallest change in your routine, habits, and patterns. Look beyond your immediate circumstances.

Begin to set goals for your future again. If you need help, ask for it. Expect the return of positive change now.

Reversed

Are you stuck in a 'lack of' mindset?

Its insidious messages creep into all areas of our lives. Want some examples? 'I suck', 'There is no one out there for me', 'I can't do anything right', 'Success is something that happens to other people', 'I'm no good with money', 'There's nothing special about me', 'Only ruthless people get ahead'... I could go on and on. Look to your inner dialogue and weed out those 'lacking' consciousness headlines when they appear. If they stem from your past, look to the source. This is fake news of the soul and the kind that nobody needs. 'Lacking' consciousness comes from lack of self-worth. You are a divine spark.

That alone makes you worthy.

SIX OF PENTACLES

Your capacity to spread compassion and wisdom to those around you is a gift. Yes, like us all you might get frustrated and annoyed at times, but fundamentally you're a giver.

The Six of Pentacles opens up your ability to receive and feel safe and rewarded for all you give. A gift is coming your way, and an act of generosity is lighting your spirit. A touch of abundance is entering, and a moment of gratitude is soothing you. You deserve to experience and feel love and abundance. Open your arms to it! Perhaps you will stumble upon someone who gives to you freely? They do this not for reward but for the pleasure of giving. How comfortable are you in receiving? Open your soul to what others have to offer you now.

On top of that, you receive the right support at the right time or perhaps you are there for a fellow soul in their time of need. Either way, a spiritual reward is on the way.

Reversed

Is your image of your own self-worth dependent on how much money you have? How you value yourself is what sets your worth, not how much you earn or your possessions. But are you judging yourself or others by what they have? Do you feel you have to 'buy your way in' to your social group by keeping up with their status symbols to belong instead of dancing together with compassion and joy like the figures in the card?

You're being asked to judge neither yourself nor your fellow souls based on their economic circumstances or what they own. It's a time of compassion, and if you are in a position to help someone or offer support, then do this. Rewards of the soul and spirit are on their way.

SEVEN OF PENTACLES

Don't give up! You are about to reap the rewards of all your hard emotional, physical, and spiritual hard work.

The Seven of Pentacles in all its lush beauty reminds us that, every so often, we need to pause the passionate pursuit of our goals and simply celebrate our magical ability to manifest. It's time to shower ourselves with praise and congratulations and to refuel with positivity.

You've reached a key stage on your success journey. At times it wasn't easy, but you committed to the long haul and you've arrived here. You're now in a position where your rewards are beginning to appear. It's not the final outcome by any means, but it's important to celebrate nonetheless.

Appreciate all you have achieved and created. Recharge and reward yourself before recommitting to the next stage.

Reversed

Fearless soul, are you ready to give up?

You may feel overwhelmed by the sheer amount of work you still have to do or that your quest is simply no longer worth the investment. You may have begun to doubt whether you're up to this task, and self-doubts are derailing you from your purpose. Who are you to think you could do this?

The answer is – only you can do this because only you have the right combination of soul strength, talent, and vision. Stay true to your vision. Take it slow and break it down.

You have what it takes.

EIGHT OF PENTACLES

It's time to use your skills in a way that benefits you and those around you. The Eight of Pentacles often sees us upskilling, starting a new job, and committing to what we do. Of course, this can include working on ourselves. How does what you do allow you to express yourself in your own individual and unique way? Because, whether you engage in paid work or not, what you do adds to your life and that of all those whose lives you touch.

If you're looking for a new career path or simply to add satisfaction and self-expression to your journey, look at what gives you a sense of fulfilment.

We all have our superpower. This card promises rewards from what you do and the way you do it.

Reversed

Does what you do fill you with passion, purpose, and enthusiasm? Do you feel you contribute in some way to bettering your life and the lives of others? Or is this all a drudge where that light is simply missing?

You may need to reboot your career or spiritual path. The Eight of Pentacles reversed tells you that your journey is about more than just working for money. Your soul wants to do more; it wants to contribute and add something.

This may not be your day job. It may be a side hustle, a creative pastime, volunteering, or another activity.

The important thing is that it adds meaning to your life and possibly to that of others too. Time to choose something more fulfilling now. Having said that, for some of us just being able to get through each day is work enough – never feel judged or down because of society's views of what 'success' is.

NINE OF PENTACLES

Abundance arrives in all its beauty and generosity. Like a person, it's here to be embraced and celebrated. Time to enjoy rewards, success, and satisfaction, and to express your gratitude. The Nine of Pentacles is a card of abundance and prosperity that you have created for yourself through your own focus, dedication, and hard work. Nobody else did this. You did it. And now you deserve to celebrate and enjoy the fruits of your achievement. Your faith in yourself has finally paid off. You've created something which has long-term potential. Sometimes this may be spiritual rather than just financial. You build new belief systems around self-worth and an abundance consciousness, and this turns into a long-term investment strategy of the soul. It allows you to access the prosperity of love, support, and meaningful work that eluded you before.

No matter how the energy of this card manifests, your spiritual strength is what got you here. Enjoy your success, soul warrior!

Reversed

You have all you need to succeed, but has your focus wavered lately?

Perhaps you've allowed yourself to be overcome with distractions or doubts? Are you scattering your talents and your energies? Reversed, this card tells you that the goal you were working so hard towards is still within reach, but you now need to re-hone that focus. Bring your energy back to it. Prioritize and don't allow self-doubt or fear of success to sway you. We all have a superpower, that area where we excel. This card asks whether you're fully utilizing yours or have overcommitted yourself. When we have an idea, we can fall into the trap of adding too much too soon. You may have to cut back that vision to really reap the rewards.

Channel that warrior strength strategically and watch how your goal takes on a life of its own again.

TEN OF PENTACLES

Lasting and well-earned rewards and security are on their way as you transform the lessons of your past and turn them into the building blocks of your future. You've shown dedication and invested in the path that held meaning for you. Your efforts have been noted. You've created a lasting legacy for yourself and others which now supports and sustains you for the long term. This card carries with it a strong sense of family Karma, not just with your family or relatives in this life but your soul family and those of other lifetimes too. If you need guidance or a helping hand, reach out to your ancestors and spirit guides. Know that you have a circle of protection around you and that the Universe is the most powerful support structure in creation. It has your back. You are and always have been part of something bigger.

Your path and purpose are set to bring rewards and recognition. Now is the time to think clearly and be practical. Time also to get serious about what it is you want and to make long-term commitments. Stay true to your path and you will be rewarded. Be seen as someone who knows what they want for their future. You're being observed, so project an authentic image, that is empowered, confident, and trustworthy. Opportunity will follow.

Reversed

The Ten of Pentacles upright is all about walking your talk and owning your purpose, and the rewards and surety which come from that. Reversed, it speaks of not learning the lessons of your past and doubting your journey.

Become a warrior for your own truth again. This is about ownership. Own your journey and what you have learned from it. Own your victories and, yes, your mistakes. Be willing to put your hand up on a soul level and say, 'I did that.' And be willing to learn from what this brought you – good or bad. Now, take all this and, with it, begin a new journey of integrity, truth, and focus.

T H E
C O U R T C A R D S

The Court cards can represent fascinating and empowering facets of all of us. Sometimes this energy can be dormant within us. When we integrate it, we literally 'rule' that area of life or the energy the Court card embodies.

Sometimes the Court cards can turn up in person. This individual may already be part of your journey. Pay close attention if someone immediately springs to mind the moment you turn a Court card over!

In other cases, someone enters our lives who perfectly reflects the personality of the card. They may come in offering a relationship, an opportunity, assistance, or, if they challenge us, a chance for growth and to learn more about ourselves. Because the Court cards always represent part of us, as we are all interconnected, all the Court cards can be any gender or non-binary; we have all of them within us.

The Tarot is one of the most powerful tools for self-actualization we know. So, whether your Court card represents an actual person or a powerful part of you that yearns to be unleashed, use its message to enhance your understanding of yourself and your relationship with those around you.

PAGE OF WANDS

Can you feel your passion rising? A rebirth and surge of energy are growing within your spirit. You are off on a new quest. Your heart craves adventure and there's the fire in your belly to go for it.

Having said that, this Tarot card is a Page. You're at the start of your journey, so you need to make sure that you don't make any rookie mistakes. You've got to grow into your magic wand, so don't get too big for your hiking boots!

You're feeling or about to feel creative, passionate, and bold. Your hunger for inspiration can only be quenched by exploring fresh possibilities.

It may be that you meet a character that embodies the Page of Wands: a young-in-age or -spirit firebrand who's open and exciting.

Reawaken your curiosity and be willing to see just where an idea could take you. Bold, daring, and proactive, the Page of Wands tells you to harness that latent potential within you and do something with your talents, ideas, and creativity.

Reversed

Is your courage buried under fear?

Did you begin a project or embark on a daring escapade only to lose your confidence or get deterred at the first sign of a setback?

It's time to get back on your horse and have faith in the truth of your wild spirit.

When the Page of Wands is reversed, it shows our best-laid plans can hit a speed bump or full reversal. But this is your journey to live in your way. The future flows around you, electrified with possibilities. Plugging back into it is easy: simply stop comparing yourself to others.

KNIGHT OF WANDS

You've probably spent some time mulling over the direction you'd like to take and now you're ready for action.

Make sure you water your horse and take care of the details, or else you could find yourself galloping into unknown territory ill-prepared. All you need to do is make a plan and add a dose of practicality to your gung-ho and effervescent new energy.

The Knight of Wands can appear as a passionate, eager, and courageous individual, adventurous, swashbuckling, and unafraid to take a chance. Their 'wow factor' fearlessness isn't faked.

It's a genuine self-belief that wins them so many hearts, admirers, and – yes – prizes. Is this an aspect of you daring you to unleash it? This Knight says, 'Go big or go home.'

There are no half measures now.

Reversed

Taking action on ideas before they are truly finished, scattering our energy, and escapism all add up to self-sabotage instead of success.

Before you go any further, the reversed Knight of Wands is asking that you stop and take stock. Are you missing something?

Guard against being impulsive. There's a big difference between this and adopting a more daring approach.

QUEEN OF WANDS

Dynamic, valorous, and bold, this courageous Queen brings the heat and lights the fire of passion within!

The Queen of Wands represents the inner firewalker. This Queen knows exactly the direction they want to head in and is fearless in their pursuit of their goal, opening their arms to the Universe and saying, 'Let's go!'

They're fiercely and rebelliously alluring and magnetic. Emboldened by desire, they play by their own rules and see life as a journey. So, what direction do you want to go in now?

The arrival of this Queen marks the start of an adventure or cycle of experience that takes you away from the mundane and into the unexplored and the new.

Take that first step with confidence and allow your free spirit to take charge.

Reversed

Have you noticed yourself getting angry or having outbursts that are out of character or happen over nothing at all? This is a sign of fire diverted or snuffed out. Your true self demands release and self-expression!

It may take courage to go looking for your life or true calling.

You may need to take a stand or leave that comfort zone behind. Reversed, this Queen tells you it's time to be brave and leave an aspect of what you know behind you.

KING

WANDS

KING OF WANDS

The King of Wands didn't start the fire – it was always burning, as the song tells us. But they fan the flames and turn up the heat.

There's no missing this King. Passionate and intense, they're extreme and extra. What you see is what you get with these charismatic and fiery creatures. Traditionally they're an Aries, Leo, or Sagittarius – intense, confident, risk-taking, and 'out there'. They crave variety and stimulation and come pre-packaged and prepared for adventure. You're in for a wild ride if one canters into your life!

This King craves variety and is always in search of the exciting and the new. Or is that you right now? Have you fallen into a rut lately, perhaps without even realizing it? If so, the energy of this card awakens your spirit of adventure and impels you to make changes or take a chance. Let's go!

Reversed

There are many paths open to us. But, reversed, the King of Wands cautions you about only exploring one. Perhaps you're passionate, but that fire and desire are directed solely at one thing or one person.

That's not healthy. Not when you have potential to burn and light up the world. Expand your horizons and send that limitless life force off to explore new areas.

PAGE

CUPS

PAGE OF CUPS

Tender spirit, step free of anything which doesn't allow that fragile inner child complete creative self-expression. Reawaken to the magic of love and enchantment as the arrival of the Page of Cups tells you it's safe to trust again.

Your heart is brought ashore, safe in your net of dreams – even if you thought these were lost for ever. Time for tender awakenings and new beginnings as this Page brings you an emotional, spiritual, or creative rebirth.

Rebirth can be a painful process as it may demand we shed ideas about ourselves, others, and what you thought you wanted from life along the way. So, this reborn version of you needs sensitive care as it takes its first tentative steps on an unknown shore.

Do you remember how you viewed the world when you were a small child? The curious magnificence of a simple shell on the beach? Approach every facet of your life anew with the same curiosity. Open your eyes to the small miracles around you, infused with the color of everyday magic.

Enjoy!

Reversed

Are you hiding from your own truth and creative brilliance?

Have you allowed cynicism to replace motivation? Maybe you dismissed your inner child with its natural affinity for playful wonder or stopped seeing your imagination as your friend, ally, and co-creator of your world? Lasting heartbreak comes from no longer believing in ourselves or our dreams. Delusion traps us into the emotional net of simply stopping trying when we fall. Look to the feelings you're neglecting – joy, fun, trust, hope, love, and happiness. Unblock whatever within you is preventing you from connecting to them.

Yes, you may have been wounded. But, reversed, the Page of Cups asks that you surrender to the process of healing.

KNIGHT OF CUPS

The most trusting and open heart is depicted in the card of the Knight of Cups: genuine, open, loyal, and overflowing with love and creative abundance.

Is this your own desire for connection embodied? If so, this card promises that your call has been answered.

What flows to you comes in the form of a sincere ambassador of love. They could manifest in the form of a lover, a deep friendship, a working connection, or a creative collaboration.

Develop the courage to be vulnerable while you wait. That takes bravery and immense trust. But you know the rewards far outweigh the risks. Being defensive or closed off keeps love at a distance.

The Knight of Cups announces clearly you will let go of any barriers that currently prevent love entering your life.

Reversed

The Knight of Cups holds a sacred chalice which represents your psychic ability. Have you been ignoring that strong soul sense around someone lately?

Perhaps they're all surface charm or, despite them saying and doing all the right things, your inner voice urges caution?

Your connection to the three Is – intuition, insight, and inspiration – form the foundations of every relationship or creative passion in your life. So, don't ignore it – or, worse, waste these gifts. Listen to what your God(dess/dex) self tells you.

Or follow the path your creative heart wants you to take. Don't ignore this. Commune with your inner wise one. Answers, truth, and a deeper love follow.

QUEEN OF CUPS

This sweet, empathic, and powerful soul gives and receives love in equal measure. Dare to open your heart chakra to its capacity to experience the full wonder of love and being loved in return.

Life takes on a luminous, more vibrant dimension when this Queen appears in a reading. Creativity, compassion, and connections are all enhanced. Someone may appear who literally makes you feel like this Queen.

But their arrival stems from your willingness to open up to a new depth of emotional truth and experience.

As always, this Court card reflects the qualities with us. The love you're experiencing now and the joy you find in this new emotional dimension were always within you. Yes, someone may appear who unlocks this for you. But this is merely to show you that your capacity to love is as boundless as the Universe you inhabit.

Reversed

Reversed, the Queen of Cups tells us that you may have been left heartbroken or drained if your capacity for love, empathy, and compassion has been taken advantage of. Worse, the reactions of others around you could have added to the wound if you have been made to feel you should 'get over it' or that you're hanging on or being oversensitive.

Own your feelings. Allow your emotional soul to self-heal by giving it permission to feel and express itself in a way that's appropriate. Avoid censoring yourself or placing a time limit on the process.

If necessary, seek out the Queen of Cups in person: a professional who acts as a guide and offers a safe environment where you can express, not repress, your feelings. Understand that cosmic love surrounds you and still lives within you. This is nothing but a temporary disconnect, no matter how long it seems to be lasting.

THE KING OF CUPS

The King of Cups has flowed into your reading today like a wave breaking on your shore, awash in all their tidal glory. They represent the element of water (their sign), are compassionate and heartfelt, and possess a deep sense of empathy and caring. Warm and kind, the King of Cups is deep and can be super sensitive.

When communicating with this King, it's important to be caring and emotionally authentic. On the shadow side, you might find that they sometimes avoid telling the truth or charm you to distort the facts.

If this card represents you, you've become much more balanced recently and are feeling emotionally secure and confident. You're learning to express yourself and know the value of your feelings. Finally, you're learning to be compassionate with yourself as well as with others, which has a miraculous effect on all your relationships.

Reversed

Are you being honest with your emotional truth? Reversed, this King poses this question and reminds us that honesty is always the way to rule when it comes to love and all our relationships. Do you feel you can only get the love you need by covert means instead of asking directly? Or that you have to hide your feeling or sugarcoat the truth as it may hurt or upset others? Yes, of course we need to consider other people's feelings. But what we should never do is hide our hurts or allow them to fester.

Reversed, the King of Cups can warn us of someone unable to operate from their heart's truth. This may be someone emotionally manipulative, unreliable, evasive, loose with the truth, or who has no respect for boundaries – either theirs or other people's. They may have addiction or commitment issues. If so, avoid any desire to 'fix' them or get sucked into their drama despite the deep empathy you may feel for them.

Understand that the best way to help them is to have clear boundaries of your own and come from your truth. Saying 'no' may turn out to be the best way to show them – and yourself – love.

PAGE OF SWORDS

Direct the wild, untamed side of your brilliance and focus your energy into positive outcomes. This Page tells you it's time to take action. But it needs to be the right action for that idea, project, or creative inspiration. Then fuel this with self-belief when it comes to seeing it through or turning that initial thought into something real.

It's time to take your ideas seriously. This Page gives you the cutting edge and the ability to get your message across to others. You go straight to the heart of the matter and won't be distracted by irrelevant issues or small talk. If this Page manifests as a person, their quicksilver mind sees opportunities or makes connections others can't fathom. Or is this you?

Writing, talking, mindfulness, and discussions feature. Dance with ideas, don't lose your divinely sent focus, and you'll turn those ideas into reality. But remember to act with your heart as well as your head, or else you could come across as childish and aggressive.

Reversed

Are you feeling a bit detached or defensive, or are you internalizing your anger so it manifests as an outward need to be right?

Sure, the snappy come-back may be on the tip of your tongue, but are you 100 per cent certain the person meant what they said to be taken that way?

And even if they did, are they really worth losing your cool over? Or just maybe your argument isn't with them – but with someone else entirely.

The Page of Swords reversed says pick your battles and think before you speak.

KNIGHT OF SWORDS

Your cutting-edge warrior spirit allows you to see both sides of any situation. This Knight brings you clarity and the right way to wield your brilliance, and recaptures your strong sense of purpose if that's been missing lately. Be careful not to use your tongue as a weapon; always step forward with kindness. Knights can represent the arrival of new situations and sometimes people, and the need to take action to address these. If it's time for action, you'll take a fearless approach but won't be reckless about it.

You've weighed up both sides of your options and factored in your outcome or how others might react. This Knight holds a sense of knowing along with their sword. They've got a strategy, a game plan. They wait for the right moment to act and won't be hurried. There's a sense of learning from past experiences. This Knight's horse represents both loyalty and a fearless spirit. The horse waits patiently for its signal and trusts the Knight will do what is right and timely.

If this Knight appears in person, if their ideas are aligned to their heart chakra, they will be prepared to fight unwaveringly on your behalf (as you may be fighting for someone or for your ideals).

Reversed

Are you allowing your true power to flow and stepping into it?

Reversed, this Knight asks whether you're being true to who you are or to your vision. Has your fear or lack of faith made you or this Knight in your life become cold-hearted and mean? Or have you or they ceased to see both sides of a situation? Heart and mind have to work together; otherwise we end up with a one-sided approach. This card reversed warns against rushing in where angels fear to tread, clinging to the need to be right, and becoming reckless or dogmatic. It warns you to be wary of anyone argumentative, sarcastic, detached, clinical, or dismissive who takes a 'my way or the highway' approach.

You may need to stand up for yourself or for others when dealing with them.

QUEEN OF SWORDS

The Queen of Swords is storming in to tell you it's time to stand your ground. Your sword is the sword of truth; it's time to hack away any BS in your life and show your strength. Perhaps you've been letting people get away with too much nonsense and your boundaries have been trampled over? Put on your armour, and say and do what's right.

On the other hand, have you become too detached from your path to see the way forward? Have you let your wounds overcome you and pulled up the drawbridge? There are many adventures still to be had and many delicious emotional experiences. Find the balance between strength, your truth and your boundaries while also stepping into the flow of love.

If this Queen appears in person, this individual has your back now. They cut to the quick when it comes to our confusion, laying bare the heart of the issue and showing you what needs to be done. Precision and strategic thinking define them. But don't make the mistake of thinking they lack heart. Just like you, they can show compassion and mercy when needed.

Reversed

Have you or someone in your life fallen into the trap of feeling you have to go it alone? Are you being overprotective of your wounds? Perhaps you come from a background where you received the message that asking for help or allowing others in is a weakness? Having good defences is one thing, but if you put up impenetrable barriers, you end up with nothing left to defend.

Put down those swords and open yourself up to others or asking for assistance. Look to past patterns in your relationships. Do you fall for people who are unavailable in order to protect yourself, for instance?

Reversed, this Queen hides a secret. And that is behind all the armour, there's a vulnerable heart in need of healing. It's time to decide if you are holding back and why. Examine your fears and make a decision. Your mind is aquiver with ideas and it's time to put them into action.

KING OF SWORDS

The King of Swords is a thinker and can appear emotionally detached.

However, sometimes we need to detach to get the job done. It's time to use your innovative and inventive ideas in a practical yet inspired way.

Become a spiritual hustler and a success story waiting to be written. Use the maverick thinkers and trailblazers who broke boundaries and a few rules to make their mark as your inspiration. Align yourself with people who walk their talk and know that you belong up there with them!

If the King of Swords appears in person, know you have the most invaluable resource within your orbit. They have the gift of cutting away anything that distracts from truth and purpose. Heed their advice and accept any help they may have to offer.

They lead by example, as you will too from this point on. However, if you want a partner/friend/lover who is soft, emotional and empathetic, this one is probably not for you.

Reversed

Reversed, the King of Swords speaks of losing your emotional heart. Or, alternatively, this may be a person whom this has happened to. Although brilliant, they may be 'all business', clinical, and devoid of empathy.

The King of Swords reversed can be a control freak and waste their brilliance. Or they refuse to see the difference between helpful and constructive feedback and criticism. This card tells you: you're smarter than that. Success is mind and soul working together. Bring back the heart into all that you do.

PAGE OF PENTACLES

The glorious Page of Pentacles is about more than simply practical matters.

The Page of Pentacles is about channeling that gleeful passion into doing what you love, and in doing so it lays the foundations for satisfaction and security.

We're not in this just for the material rewards, although Pentacles are often misinterpreted in this way. The bigger takeaway could just be the pleasure we get from doing something well, or doing a job that doesn't just feed the body but feeds the soul too. Or building on our sense of security, be that emotional, physical, or spiritual.

Is it time to upgrade your soul path? In doing so, you'll take those baby steps towards increased satisfaction and security. The Page of Pentacles says explore it with the wide-eyed enthusiasm of the child within you.

Reversed

Maybe you did once enjoy what you were doing. But satisfaction and pleasure left the building a long time ago, didn't they? Isn't it time to own that?

If you no longer love what you do – or never did for that matter – the Page of Pentacles reversed tells you to look at how to recapture your inner purpose or simply pleasure in your path.

Maybe you need to step back and look at all your options – which could be more than you believe are open to you! Are you simply burned out or being childishly stubborn?

Or are you ignoring the call of your inventive soul? Take practical steps to emotionally supporting yourself.

KNIGHT OF PENTACLES

This Knight has incredible resources at their disposal. Creative, earthy, determined, and committed, the appearance of the Knight of Pentacles asks you to tame your potential and harness your resources.

But they also ask you to know that there are going to be no short cuts when it comes to what you want to achieve. Grounded, practical, and stable, this Knight is in it for the long haul.

Dedicate your soul to your goal now. Be prepared to go the distance. This Knight speaks of skills that have taken a long time to perfect and of working with what you have in a practical manner, not allowing any opportunity to escape.

Talented with all things practical and other resources, the Knight of Pentacles asks you to utilize your past experiences and use them to develop your talents and reimagine your future.

It's all about deferred gratification.

Reversed

Nothing ventured, nothing gained. Reversed, the Knight of Pentacles can have us stuck and unwilling to take a chance.

We may have become so fixated on one outcome that we miss out on alternatives, stubbornly insist on repeating the same cycle again and again while expecting a different result, or cling on to the past like a parrot with a cuttlebone.

You are more inventive and flexible than you imagine. Your soul is not set in stone; it is an ever-changing facet of light. This Knight reversed is asking that you try a fresh approach. Or to redefine what success means to you.

QUEEN OF PENTACLES

Joyful in their sensuality and ability to experience abundance, the Queen of Pentacles is the Queen who rules the material world with practicality, gratitude, and appreciation.

It's time to build on your curiosity and ground your imagination. You have a very tenacious spirit and you will never give up or give in. However, if the Queen of Pentacles commits to a course of action, they find it very difficult to switch plans.

To be a real Queen of our destiny, we have to be a spiritual sprite and be able to change track at any point. When we're flexible with our will, we can achieve and grow beyond our expectations.

Hone your skills and trust your warrior heart. Use your intuition to guide where you focus your energy and what to build on. You could meet another Queen who will help show you the way.

Grounded and sensual, this Queen appreciates beauty, art, nature, and the good things of life. They understand that these are ways of honoring the self and others, and that they form an important part of our spiritual experience. The arrival of the Queen of Pentacles tells you that your time of success and harvest approaches.

Reversed

What is causing you to doubt yourself? Is worry diverting you from your purpose? Or are you stubbornly sticking to a course of action that is clearly not working for you? Although blessed with the determination of long-term vision, the Queen of Pentacles reversed can be susceptible to outside influences which cause anxiety and self-doubt to derail their path.

Do you doubt your ability to create the security you need? It's time to own your power and to trust your innate abilities and gifts. Begin by focusing gratitude on what you already have and use your intuition to guide your focus and show you where to send your energy and what to build on.

KING OF PENTACLES

This King understands that, if you control your inner resources, you control your outer world. Grounded, sensual, loyal, and hard-working, this King (and remember, Court cards are all genders or gender neutral and non-binary) represents reliability, strength, a connection to nature, and worldly success but not at the expense of sacrificing what truly matters.

If this King manifests in human form, they will appear as someone successful (not necessarily in the patriarchal sense, but whatever success means to you) and someone who keeps their word.

The King of Pentacles' energy that lives within hands you the ability to control your resources and your reality. You are able to take whatever practical steps are needed to achieve your goals. What's more, you now understand that your most valuable assets are commitment and patience. Nothing pays off like persistence when it comes to success.

Reversed

Stubborn, stuck, single-minded, the King of Pentacles reversed shows us someone clinging to an idea, routine, or way of doing things that has long ago lost its purpose.

At their very worst, the reversed King of Pentacles appears as someone with delusions of grandeur, a narcissist, or a snob. They may project a sense of self-entitlement and want success and the rewards that come with that, but be unwilling to work for them.

You, steadfast soul, have been making an effort. But, reversed, the King of Pentacles asks whether there is a another, better way to attain the results you're seeking. It asks you to tap into flexibility, to experiment and explore a new approach, and to reawaken within the sheer pleasure of mastering something fresh and new. Redefine what success means to you now.

SAMPLE SPREADS

The only limit on how to conduct a Tarot reading is your imagination! As you get familiar with the cards, you will begin to create your own spreads that allow you to ask different questions of the Tarot depending on your personal situation. For now, though, I've included two basic spreads to get you started.

For each I've given an explanation of what it is and how to use it, and I've included journalling space with prompts for you to record your reactions.

ONE-CARD READING

A fabulous use of the cards is the daily practice of pulling one card to bring a message about your day. You can also ask a question and be guided by the card you pull, bringing profound insights into your life.

So let's dive in. The first step is to hold the deck face down in your hand and select a card. Take a moment to connect with it. Look at it deeply and pay attention to any thoughts that come up and what feelings it inspires. Write them down on the following pages. Allow yourself to flow with the ideas that come through and write them down without questioning or editing yourself.

Allow yourself to focus on the deeper meaning of the card. You may begin to notice connections between the colors, symbols, backgrounds, or people depicted in the card.

The second step is to consider the card's interpretation and how it applies to your question. All of this provides a useful starting point for your reading. Have faith in your magical being. You have a deep pool of intuitive knowledge that the Tarot can release.

The third and most important step is to draw out all the hidden information from your card and apply it to your current situation. Tarot is very personal. What do the colors or images mean to you? This is where you can really start to have a conversation with the card, which is how we form a relationship with our deck.

Ask yourself what the card says about the key areas of your life: love, work, money, health, and spirituality. Write down everything you feel applies to each area, even if your question was about only one or none.

Once you have completed these three steps, you may have your answer. If your question doesn't fit into the five key areas, don't worry. This process has opened up your intuition and allowed you to obtain an answer from the card. Record all of your impressions and answers in your journal so you can refer back to them.

It's incredible how much information one card can offer across all areas of your life. With this simple technique, you have the power of the Tarot at your fingertips in a dynamic one-card reading. Be bold and use this technique for all sorts of questions. You'll be amazed at the accuracy of the answers you can get.

Date: ———————————

Card:

Did you have a specific question in mind when you pulled the card, and if so, what was it?

_____

_____

_____

_____

What is your response to the card? What thoughts come to you and what feelings does it inspire?

_____

_____

_____

_____

What does the card's interpretation tell you generally, or specifically in relation to your question? What do the colors or images mean to you?

_____

_____

_____

_____

_____

What does the card say about the key areas of your life: love, work, money, health, and spirituality?

_____

_____

_____

_____

_____

Has this process given you a message about your day or an answer to your question? Record it here along with any other thoughts or impressions.

_____

_____

_____

_____

_____

Date: _____

Card:

Did you have a specific question in mind when you pulled the card, and if so, what was it?

_____

_____

_____

_____

What is your response to the card? What thoughts come to you and what feelings does it inspire?

_____

_____

_____

_____

What does the card's interpretation tell you generally, or specifically in relation to your question? What do the colors or images mean to you?

_____

_____

_____

_____

_____

What does the card say about the key areas of your life: love, work, money, health, and spirituality?

_____

_____

_____

_____

_____

Has this process given you a message about your day or an answer to your question? Record it here along with any other thoughts or impressions.

_____

_____

_____

_____

_____

Date: _____

Card:

Did you have a specific question in mind when you pulled the card, and if so, what was it?

_____

_____

_____

_____

What is your response to the card? What thoughts come to you and what feelings does it inspire?

_____

_____

_____

_____

What does the card's interpretation tell you generally, or specifically in relation to your question? What do the colors or images mean to you?

_____

_____

_____

_____

_____

What does the card say about the key areas of your life: love, work, money, health, and spirituality?

_____

_____

_____

_____

_____

Has this process given you a message about your day or an answer to your question? Record it here along with any other thoughts or impressions.

_____

_____

_____

_____

_____

Date: ───────────────

Card:

Did you have a specific question in mind when you pulled the card, and if so, what was it?

_____

_____

_____

_____

What is your response to the card? What thoughts come to you and what feelings does it inspire?

_____

_____

_____

_____

What does the card's interpretation tell you generally, or specifically in relation to your question? What do the colors or images mean to you?

_____

_____

_____

_____

_____

What does the card say about the key areas of your life: love, work, money, health, and spirituality?

_____

_____

_____

_____

Has this process given you a message about your day or an answer to your question? Record it here along with any other thoughts or impressions.

_____

_____

_____

_____

Date: ————————————

Card:

Did you have a specific question in mind when you pulled the card, and if so, what was it?

_____

_____

_____

_____

What is your response to the card? What thoughts come to you and what feelings does it inspire?

_____

_____

_____

_____

What does the card's interpretation tell you generally, or specifically in relation to your question? What do the colors or images mean to you?

_____

_____

_____

_____

_____

What does the card say about the key areas of your life: love, work, money, health, and spirituality?

_____

_____

_____

_____

Has this process given you a message about your day or an answer to your question? Record it here along with any other thoughts or impressions.

_____

_____

_____

_____

_____

Date: _____

Card:

Did you have a specific question in mind when you pulled the card, and if so, what was it?

_____

_____

_____

_____

What is your response to the card? What thoughts come to you and what feelings does it inspire?

_____

_____

_____

_____

What does the card's interpretation tell you generally, or specifically in relation to your question? What do the colors or images mean to you?

_____

_____

_____

_____

_____

What does the card say about the key areas of your life: love, work, money, health, and spirituality?

_____

_____

_____

_____

_____

Has this process given you a message about your day or an answer to your question? Record it here along with any other thoughts or impressions.

_____

_____

_____

_____

_____

Date: ──────────────

Card:

Did you have a specific question in mind when you pulled the card, and if so, what was it?

──

──

──

──

What is your response to the card? What thoughts come to you and what feelings does it inspire?

──

──

──

──

What does the card's interpretation tell you generally, or specifically in relation to your question? What do the colors or images mean to you?

_____

_____

_____

_____

_____

What does the card say about the key areas of your life: love, work, money, health, and spirituality?

_____

_____

_____

_____

_____

Has this process given you a message about your day or an answer to your question? Record it here along with any other thoughts or impressions.

_____

_____

_____

_____

_____

Date: _____

Card:

Did you have a specific question in mind when you pulled the card, and if so, what was it?

_____

_____

_____

_____

What is your response to the card? What thoughts come to you and what feelings does it inspire?

_____

_____

_____

_____

What does the card's interpretation tell you generally, or specifically in relation to your question? What do the colors or images mean to you?

_____

_____

_____

_____

_____

What does the card say about the key areas of your life: love, work, money, health, and spirituality?

_____

_____

_____

_____

_____

Has this process given you a message about your day or an answer to your question? Record it here along with any other thoughts or impressions.

_____

_____

_____

_____

_____

Date: —————————————

Card:

Did you have a specific question in mind when you pulled the card, and if so, what was it?

_____

_____

_____

_____

What is your response to the card? What thoughts come to you and what feelings does it inspire?

_____

_____

_____

_____

What does the card's interpretation tell you generally, or specifically in relation to your question? What do the colors or images mean to you?

_____

_____

_____

_____

_____

What does the card say about the key areas of your life: love, work, money, health, and spirituality?

_____

_____

_____

_____

Has this process given you a message about your day or an answer to your question? Record it here along with any other thoughts or impressions.

_____

_____

_____

_____

_____

Date: ———————————

Card:

Did you have a specific question in mind when you pulled the card, and if so, what was it?

_____

_____

_____

_____

What is your response to the card? What thoughts come to you and what feelings does it inspire?

_____

_____

_____

_____

What does the card's interpretation tell you generally, or specifically in relation to your question? What do the colors or images mean to you?

_____

_____

_____

_____

_____

What does the card say about the key areas of your life: love, work, money, health, and spirituality?

_____

_____

_____

_____

Has this process given you a message about your day or an answer to your question? Record it here along with any other thoughts or impressions.

_____

_____

_____

_____

_____

Date: _____

Card:

Did you have a specific question in mind when you pulled the card, and if so, what was it?

_____

_____

_____

_____

What is your response to the card? What thoughts come to you and what feelings does it inspire?

_____

_____

_____

_____

What does the card's interpretation tell you generally, or specifically in relation to your question? What do the colors or images mean to you?

_____

_____

_____

_____

_____

What does the card say about the key areas of your life: love, work, money, health, and spirituality?

_____

_____

_____

_____

_____

Has this process given you a message about your day or an answer to your question? Record it here along with any other thoughts or impressions.

_____

_____

_____

_____

_____

THE SIX STEPS OF INSIGHT

There's no doubt that the Tarot is a powerful tool of divination and transformation. But the uses of Tarot cards go far beyond just looking at how the future may unfold. Tarot cards can be used to unlock insights into ourselves and others, and allow us to transform our future. What's more, you don't need to be a Tarot expert or consult a professional reader to do this. You can use your Tarot deck whether you understand all the traditional meanings of the cards or not. It's a simple but liberating technique that I call the Six Steps of Insight.

Step One

First of all, let go of all the traditional interpretations of the cards before you start this exercise. We aren't going to interpret the cards but connect with them on a soul resonance level. This requires us to let go of any desire to predict outcomes or overlay the cards with what we may want to happen. If you don't know how to interpret the cards – congratulations! There will be no preconceptions to hamper you.

Step Two

Now lay out your entire Tarot deck FACE UP in front of you. You can lay them out in any order just as they come out of the pack. You do not have to put all the major arcana or suits together.

Once you have done this, sit back and allow your eyes to take in your entire deck. Again, don't think about the meaning of the cards; allow other impressions to form – the colors and the feelings the images evoke in you.

Step Three

After you have 'sat' with your cards for a few moments, I want you to choose the six cards you are most drawn to and like. Again, for this exercise to work, your choice needs to be based on your impressions of the cards, the feelings they evoke in you, the colors and images you are most drawn to and resonate with, as opposed to what you might want to happen in your life. You may want a new love to come into your life but don't pick the Lovers or the Two of Cups just because of that. Go with your instincts.

Step Four

Now – choose the six cards you like the least! Perhaps your choice here is influenced by dark colors, images of difficulty or sleepless nights. Or you discover that for some reason right now you really don't like a card that is otherwise light, bright and positive. If that's the case – and it can be – then add it to your least liked. Remember, this is all about how you feel about the cards, not about their meaning per se.

Step Five

Arrange your six 'likes' in a row and your six 'dislikes' underneath them.

Likes

Dislikes

Look at them closely. Do any of the cards you have selected as a 'like' have a clear opposite – a card in the 'dislike' row that evokes the opposite feeling in you to your 'like'? If so, arrange them so one is above the other. You may find that you have unconsciously selected more than one pair of cards representing the opposite. Again, place them so one is above the other. Also look to see if the cards are telling a 'story' in some way. Is there a link you can see between them? If so, arrange them again so the story unfolds in a linear fashion.

Step Six

Finally, once again letting go of any traditional interpretations of the cards, do these cards remind you of anyone or anything that has been or is going on in your life right now? Again, this is all about your 'gut' reaction to your chosen cards and the thoughts and feelings they evoke.

You may have chosen the Three of Swords and this leads you to the insight that, despite the fact you are now dating, you still have some processing to do to get over your previous relationship.

Write down the cards you have chosen and any insights that come through for you about why you have chosen them and what they represent for you on an emotional and psychic level. You may find that you have picked some cards that appear to have no bearing on anything that is going on for you. These can be the most interesting of all as you will have usually picked them for a reason. Again, write down what you believe the card could represent for you.

Repeat When Needed

This exercise can be a powerful tool for gaining insight and handy for anyone wanting to hone their Tarot skills, whether a complete beginner or a professional reader, as it enables you to link your subconscious mind to the cards and draw amazing insights from them.

As time passes, you may be amazed, when you reread what you wrote regarding your choices, how accurate your emotional connection and interpretation were. You can be your own Tarot reader!

Repeat this exercise whenever you require insight into what is happening in your life or what may be coming up. The interesting thing is that you will choose different cards every time, but your interpretation of the cards makes this exercise such a powerful tool of insight and empowerment.

Date: _____

Selections:

Likes

Dislikes

What made you choose your six likes? What feelings did the cards evoke in you? What insights do you have about why you chose them and what they could represent?

_____

_____

What made you choose your six dislikes? What feelings did the cards evoke in you? What insights do you have about why you chose them and what they could represent?

_____

_____

What 'opposites' did you arrange above and below each other and why?

_____

_____

_____

_____

_____

_____

What changes to the order of the cards did you make so that they could tell their story and what is that story?

_____

_____

_____

_____

_____

_____

Do these cards remind you of anyone or anything that has been or is going on in your life right now?

_____

_____

_____

_____

_____

_____

Date: _____

Selections:

Likes

Dislikes

What made you choose your six likes? What feelings did the cards evoke in you? What insights do you have about why you chose them and what they could represent?

_____

_____

What made you choose your six dislikes? What feelings did the cards evoke in you? What insights do you have about why you chose them and what they could represent?

_____

_____

What 'opposites' did you arrange above and below each other and why?

_____

_____

_____

_____

_____

_____

What changes to the order of the cards did you make so that they could tell their story and what is that story?

_____

_____

_____

_____

_____

_____

Do these cards remind you of anyone or anything that has been or is going on in your life right now?

_____

_____

_____

_____

_____

Date: _____

Selections:

Likes

☐ ☐ ☐ ☐ ☐ ☐

Dislikes

☐ ☐ ☐ ☐ ☐ ☐

What made you choose your six likes? What feelings did the cards evoke in you? What insights do you have about why you chose them and what they could represent?

_____

_____

What made you choose your six dislikes? What feelings did the cards evoke in you? What insights do you have about why you chose them and what they could represent?

_____

_____

What 'opposites' did you arrange above and below each other and why?

_____

_____

_____

_____

_____

What changes to the order of the cards did you make so that they could tell their story and what is that story?

_____

_____

_____

_____

_____

Do these cards remind you of anyone or anything that has been or is going on in your life right now?

_____

_____

_____

_____

_____

Date: _____

Selections:

Likes

Dislikes

What made you choose your six likes? What feelings did the cards evoke in you? What insights do you have about why you chose them and what they could represent?

_____

_____

What made you choose your six dislikes? What feelings did the cards evoke in you? What insights do you have about why you chose them and what they could represent?

_____

_____

What 'opposites' did you arrange above and below each other and why?

_____

_____

_____

_____

_____

_____

What changes to the order of the cards did you make so that they could tell their story and what is that story?

_____

_____

_____

_____

_____

_____

Do these cards remind you of anyone or anything that has been or is going on in your life right now?

_____

_____

_____

_____

_____

_____

Date: _____

Selections:

Likes

Dislikes

What made you choose your six likes? What feelings did the cards evoke in you? What insights do you have about why you chose them and what they could represent?

_____

_____

What made you choose your six dislikes? What feelings did the cards evoke in you? What insights do you have about why you chose them and what they could represent?

_____

_____

What 'opposites' did you arrange above and below each other and why?

_____

_____

_____

_____

_____

What changes to the order of the cards did you make so that they could tell their story and what is that story?

_____

_____

_____

_____

_____

Do these cards remind you of anyone or anything that has been or is going on in your life right now?

_____

_____

_____

_____

_____

Date: _____

Selections:

Likes

Dislikes

What made you choose your six likes? What feelings did the cards evoke in you? What insights do you have about why you chose them and what they could represent?

_____

_____

What made you choose your six dislikes? What feelings did the cards evoke in you? What insights do you have about why you chose them and what they could represent?

_____

_____

What 'opposites' did you arrange above and below each other and why?

_____

_____

_____

_____

_____

What changes to the order of the cards did you make so that they could tell their story and what is that story?

_____

_____

_____

_____

_____

Do these cards remind you of anyone or anything that has been or is going on in your life right now?

_____

_____

_____

_____

_____

Date: _____

Selections:

Likes

Dislikes

What made you choose your six likes? What feelings did the cards evoke in you? What insights do you have about why you chose them and what they could represent?

_____

_____

What made you choose your six dislikes? What feelings did the cards evoke in you? What insights do you have about why you chose them and what they could represent?

_____

_____

What 'opposites' did you arrange above and below each other and why?

_____

_____

_____

_____

_____

_____

What changes to the order of the cards did you make so that they could tell their story and what is that story?

_____

_____

_____

_____

_____

Do these cards remind you of anyone or anything that has been or is going on in your life right now?

_____

_____

_____

_____

_____

Date: _____

Selections:

Likes

Dislikes

What made you choose your six likes? What feelings did the cards evoke in you? What insights do you have about why you chose them and what they could represent?

_____

_____

What made you choose your six dislikes? What feelings did the cards evoke in you? What insights do you have about why you chose them and what they could represent?

_____

_____

What 'opposites' did you arrange above and below each other and why?

_____

_____

_____

_____

_____

_____

What changes to the order of the cards did you make so that they could tell their story and what is that story?

_____

_____

_____

_____

_____

_____

Do these cards remind you of anyone or anything that has been or is going on in your life right now?

_____

_____

_____

_____

_____

_____

OUR TAROT SUPERSTARS

These empowering, magical beings paved the way for our freedoms –
dazzling souls who changed the world – and yet many of them never got
the true recognition they deserved. I feel so honored to have them in this
deck. May these magical and magnificent spirits shine eternally on.

THE HIGH PRIESTESS
PAMELA COLMAN-SMITH

THE HIGH PRIESTESS

'Note the dress, the type of face; see if you can trace the character in the face; note the pose. ... First watch the simple forms of joy, of fear, of sorrow; look at the position taken by the whole body. ... After you have found how to tell a simple story, put in more details. ... Learn from everything, see everything, and above all feel everything! ... Find eyes within, look for the door into the unknown country.'

Visionary Aquarius with Mercury in Aquarius and fierce Moon in Leo, Pamela Colman-Smith is the forgotten illustrator who created the Rider–Waite Tarot images in 1912. Fondly nicknamed Pixie, her bright spirit was a creative whirl of wonder. Probably a lesbian/queer and certainly a Suffragette and a member of the Golden Dawn, she was born to a Jamaican mother and white American father. She was great friends with famous lesbian Edith Craig who was the model for the face of the Queen of Wands. Colman-Smith spent 40 years living with her partner and fellow spiritualist Nora Lake. In later life, they opened a retreat for Catholic priests in Cornwall. Pixie started off as a set designer and then an illustrator for W. B. Yeats, Bram Stoker, and others. Despite creating the images for what became the most popular Tarot deck of all time, she wrote a letter saying how little she was paid for it and never earned royalties, dying virtually penniless. We owe an everlasting debt of gratitude to this magical pioneer, artist, and extraordinary soul who gave us the gift of the most profound and successful Tarot deck in the world.

THE HIEROPHANT

W. E. B. DU BOIS

'Now is the accepted time, not tomorrow, not some more convenient season. It is today that our best work can be done and not some future day or future year.'

Our Hierophant, the incredible civil rights activist W. E. B. Du Bois, challenged and changed society, refusing to give in to the tyranny enclosing him. He is a testament to the power an individual can have in the wider community. He is considered the most important Black protest leader in the United States during the first half of the 20th century.

A sociologist and scholar who wrote the first significant case study of African Americans in the United States, he was the leader of the Niagara Movement, a group of African American activists fighting for equal rights. He was also the first African American to earn a PhD from Harvard. Du Bois fiercely strived to wipe out racism and was also a staunch advocate of women's rights, and remains an unsung hero whose lifelong vision helped change the world and millions of lives for the better.

THE CHARIOT

AIDA OVERTON WALKER

'Unless we learn the lesson of self-appreciation and practice it, we shall spend our lives imitating other people and deprecating ourselves.'

The outstanding Aquarius visionary Aida Overton-Walker was born on Valentine's Day in 1880. She was a performer, choreographer, comedian, activist, and superstar, billed as the 'Queen of the cake walk'. She was a true trailblazer who shattered all stereotypes. Refusing to play racist and demeaning roles, Overton-Walker was the first African American to play Carnegie Hall and the first Black actor to headline in vaudeville. Every step she took in life she did her way. Not only did she take the time to pour love and energy into her art, but she also gave this same care and passion to her community. Her courageous, inspirational spirit refused to let the social conventions of the time confine her creativity and political beliefs. Instead, she smashed down barriers and refused to compromise. Establishing her own vaudeville company, she created a Black cultural identity onstage that was unheard of in this era, paving the way for other artists. Overton-Walker is also considered one of the first drag kings, as, after her husband died, she wore drag in her shows to play his roles. A command performance at Buckingham Palace sealed her reputation as the first international Black superstar. She tragically died of kidney disease at the age of 34. She is the perfect Chariot, as the force of her brilliance, will, power, and charisma helped her drive through every obstacle to reach her dreams.

THE HERMIT

ANNA MAY WONG

'Why is it that the screen Chinese is always the villain? And so crude a villain – murderous, treacherous, a snake in the grass! We are not like that. How could we be, with a civilization that is so many times older than the West?'

Born 3 January 1905, Anna Mae Wong was a tenacious Capricorn with a free-spirited Moon in Sagittarius. Our Hermit had the heroism to listen to her own wisdom and follow her inner soul compass. The legendary Wong was the first Chinese international superstar and style icon. A forgotten hero, she challenged the horrendous racism of Hollywood and fought for the positive portrayal of Chinese actors on screen. Rather than buy into racist casting that constantly portrayed Asians as the villain, she turned down leading roles to avoid perpetuating racist stereotypes.

Our heroine, tired of non-Asian actors being cast as Chinese leads, left Hollywood for Europe where she achieved international stardom in the British film *Piccadilly*. However, an alleged torrid love affair with Marlene Dietrich damaged her public image.

She returned to the United States where Hollywood offered her lead roles, but ones which continued only to be stereotypes. Eventually, her ability to stay true to her own inner light paid off and Anna Mae became the first Chinese actor to have their own TV show – *The Gallery of Madame Liu-Tsong*.

TEMPERANCE

MARIA MONTEZ

The stuff that dreams are made of, our Temperance Gemini goddess superstar with 'don't mess with me' Mars in Leo, Maria Montez, is the epitome of authenticity and cosmic flow. Born María África Gracia Vidal, she was a Dominican actor dubbed the 'Queen of Technicolor' due to her roles in a series of glamorous films, in which she wowed Hollywood with a mix of old-fashioned stardom and free-spirited independence. Married at 17, she soon ditched her wealthy husband to pursue her own path. Maria blasted into fame following her lead in *The Invisible Woman* and *Arabian Nights*. In real life, she was just as adventurous as the characters she portrayed. Her second husband, French actor Jean-Pierre Aumont, wrote of her: 'An astrologer, a physical culture expert, a priest, a cook, and two masseurs were part of the furnishings. During her massage sessions, Montez granted audiences.' Maria battled racism and even her studio, Universal, in order to have her name spelled correctly. Universal wanted a 'z', and sadly it got its way. Despite this, she took no crap and sued Universal for not giving her star billing, a suit which was settled out of court. A great believer in astrology, she was told by a famous astrologer, Madam Blanca Holmes, that she would die young. She drowned in a hot bath when she suffered a heart attack brought on by heat stroke at her home in France, aged 39.

THE STAR

MATA HARI

'My dance is a sacred poem in which each movement is a word and whose every word is underlined by music. The temple in which I dance can be vague or faithfully reproduced, for I am the temple.'

Her name immortalized for being a famous courtesan, dancer, and double agent, Mata Hari was a wild and free-spirited woman in charge of her sexuality who slept with whom she wanted. She courageously left her first, abusive husband and reinvented herself. From the ashes of her old life, Mata Hari was born. She rebranded herself many times* finally becoming famous as an erotic dancer known for her Dance of the Seven Veils (taken from the Babylonian myth of the Goddess Ishtar). Her huge Leo maverick, confident, rebel persona, coupled with being sexually free in a time when it was dangerous to do so, brought her many enemies. After taking lovers from both sides during World War I, she was declared a spy. It was perfect timing to scapegoat her for the French failures on the Western Front. Held up as a she-devil, Mata Hari's prosecutor, Pierre Bouchardon, focused not on her actions but on her character: 'Without scruples, accustomed to make use of men, she is the type of woman who is born to be a spy.' Convicted without a shred of evidence in a travesty of a court riven with misogyny, she was sentenced to death. Mata Hari died by firing squad in 1917. Fiercely courageous to the very end, she refused a blindfold and held her head high.

'I am a woman who enjoys herself very much; sometimes I lose, sometimes I win.'

* Mata Hari has always been problematic. Some of her more outrageous stories – such as being the daughter of an Indian temple dancer – would be considered cultural appropriation today.

THE MOON

BESSIE SMITH

'I don't need no drummer. I set the tempo.'

'Empress of the Blues' Bessie Smith is famous for her big voice and extraordinary charismatic performances. She started performing when she was nine after both her parents died. She suffered immensely, experiencing extreme poverty, and was busking for pennies just to survive.

A visionary, powerful Aries, in 1913 she toured with another queer performer, Ma Rainey, through whom she gained much of her inspiration. She soon became the most popular and best-paid blues singer of the 1920s. Bessie made 160 recordings for Columbia Records (which treated her appallingly) and sold six million records in four years. Never one to accept any nonsense, Bessie once famously chased the KKK out of one of her performances, telling them they'd better take their sheets and run (which they did).

At the height of her fame, Bessie bought her own train carriage, and this gave her the freedom to express herself, to move around without dealing with segregation and other racist oppression, and to hold outrageous parties. Bessie did nothing by halves. She was openly bisexual, bold, and a total genius, all while being true to herself.

Sadly, she died aged 48 in a car accident.

'Listen to my story and everything will come out true.'

223

SEVEN OF WANDS

SYLVIA PANKHURST

Taurus Suffragette Sylvia Pankhurst was the daughter of Emmeline Pankhurst and sister to Christabel. She dedicated her life to equality and making a difference. All three were part of the militant Suffragette organization that used fearless tactics, to draw attention to their cause. The Pankhursts were arrested numerous times, enduring imprisonment and force-feeding while on hunger strike. Ultimately, their tactics paid off, and women over 30 got the vote in 1918, and in 1928 women over 21.

While there has been much (valid) debate about racism in the Suffragette movement, with criticism of the Pankhursts' focus on white, middle-class women and their lack of support for racial and economic justice issues. Silvia was different. Sylvia moved away from her mother and sister to focus on working-class women and fight colonialism. In the 1930s, Sylvia turned her focus to the anti-fascist movement. In 1935, enraged by Italy's invasion of Ethiopia, she campaigned tirelessly to bring it to the attention of the British government. She worked with Haile Selassie, who invited her to live in Ethiopia, where she died, honored by the Ethiopian emperor for her dedication to activism.

She shows us the true meaning of the Seven of Wands: never give up as, even if you can't see it, you are winning.

SEVEN OF SWORDS

BARONESS ELSA VON FREYTAG-LORINGHOVEN

'*Do what you will! This world's your oyster, Pet. But be forewarned. The sea might drown you yet.*'

Gender fluid, queer and bisexual, Baroness Elsa von Freytag-Loringhoven was a cosmic Cancerian who should rightly be considered the founder of the Dada movement, but whose role has been minimized due to patriarchal gender bias.

An 'eccentric maverick', the baroness was once arrested for walking down Fifth Avenue while wearing a man's suit and smoking a cigarette – cross-dressing was illegal at the time. Baroness Elsa lived via art and self-expression and became a walking creation of it, dressing with tin cans for bras and sporting a bird cage with a live bird for a hat, taking joy in discarded items and seeing unborn creative potential in trash.

Arguably Dada's most famous artwork, *The Fountain*, was allegedly Elsa's and was 'stolen' and attributed to Marcel Duchamp, one of the key figures of Dadaism. Today, art historians agree that the evidence points to Elsa being the artist, but Duchamp took credit for it after she died – hence the connection with something being stolen from us associated with this card. Baroness Elsa, we salute you.

KING OF SWORDS

OSCAR WILDE

'*We are all in the gutter, but some of us are looking at the stars.*'

Glittering, gloriously decadent, and wildly queer, our King of Swords is fittingly a Libran. Born 16 October 1854, Oscar Wilde lived a life of extravagant genius and hedonistic creativity. Easily one of the greatest minds in human history, the author of *The Importance of Being Earnest* and *The Picture of Dorian Gray* is known for his incredible wit and pithy aphorisms. He was a playwright, novelist, and poet and had a rapier-sharp mind, casually dropping legendary quotations wherever he went (a personal favourite of mine is 'I can resist anything except temptation'). The King of Swords knows instinctively that words and ideas can make us immortal.

Oscar Wilde is without doubt an essential part of queer history, not because he was publicly gay (in fact, his downfall came from suing the Marquess of Queensberry for calling him a sodomite) but, because at the time, he was a superstar. With his long hair, flamboyant style of dress, and love of beauty, Wilde lived his life as a work of art of his own creation. His trial and subsequent jailing for 'gross indecency' brought queerness into the mainstream. Even after two horrendous years of hard labour in jail, his final years in France saw him as an equally passionate campaigner for prison reform. In 2017, he was posthumously pardoned. His legend lives on, as does his mark on queer history.

'*Be yourself; everyone else is already taken.*'

THE WORLD

SISTER ROSETTA THARPE

'Can't no man play like me.'

Our World card is the original rocker of worlds. Who knew that the originator of rock and roll was a queer Black woman who blew the music industry apart? Often known as 'The Godmother of Rock and Roll' and original soul sister, she pioneered the electric guitar, her distinct style influencing generations. Her guitar solos and riffs were a unique inspiration, dazzling audiences everywhere and giving birth to the future of electric guitar music.

She blended elements of blues and jazz in her music, creating a unique sound ahead of its time. Her performances were electrifying, and she was known for her raw power, flashy outfits, and willingness to take risks on stage. Spiritual Pisces Sister Rosetta released her first record in 1938 with Decca, 'Rock Me'. It was an instant hit and is now considered the inspiration for the launch of rock and roll (many years later!).

Beginning in gospel shows and on radio programs, Sister Rosetta was one of the most popular and respected musicians in the gospel world. Her decision to perform in nightclubs was controversial. Some members of the gospel community believed that Sister Rosetta was compromising her faith by performing in them. Couple this with her 'rumoured' (translate to 'open secret') long-term relationship with musician Marie Knight with whom she toured for many years, and it's clear that she always chose to do things her way!

ACKNOWLEDGEMENTS

Deep gratitude to a dear friend and long-time collaborator, one of the best astrologers and psychics I know, Helen Harvey Watts. She not only edited this, but shared her incredible insights as she pushed, cajoled, and threw me over the line to get it finished.

To my designer, Flor Rangel, who is a genius. My eternal gratitude for your bright brilliance and for sharing the journey with me.

To my son, Julien, who I am hoping will carry the love of Tarot into the next generation (hint, hint!).

And to you, dear reader, for supporting this labour of love.

Much love and magic,

Michele Knight-Waite

LYNDELL MANSFIELD

10TH MARCH 1972 - 1ST OCTOBER 2021

IN LOVING MEMORY OF MY SOUL SISTER

the enchanting, bewitching, kind, original, unique Pisces punk Mutha Goddess

LYNDELL MANSFIELD

She contained the magic of all the Tarot cards.

*She's dancing in a different dimension, yet we carry
her in our spirit for eternity.*

DISCOVER THE OFFICIAL
KNIGHT-WAITE TAROT DECK